the **art** of **explanation**

the art of
explanation

making your ideas, products, and services easier to understand

LEE LEFEVER

WILEY

John Wiley & Sons, Inc.

Cover image: Courtesy of Lee LeFever
Cover design: C. Wallace

This book is printed on acid-free paper.∞

Copyright © 2013 by Lee LeFever. All rights reserved.

Published by John Wiley & Sons, Inc., Hoboken, New Jersey.
Published simultaneously in Canada.

For general information on our other products and services or for technical support, please contact our Customer Care Department within the United States at (800) 762-2974, outside the United States at (317) 572-3993 or fax (317) 572-4002.

Wiley publishes in a variety of print and electronic formats and by print-on-demand. Some material included with standard print versions of this book may not be included in e-books or in print-on-demand. If this book refers to media such as a CD or DVD that is not included in the version you purchased, you may download this material at http://booksupport.wiley.com. For more information about Wiley products, visit www.wiley.com.

Library of Congress Cataloging-in-Publication Data:
LeFever, Lee, 1973–
  Art of explanation : making your ideas, products, and services easier to
understand / Lee LeFever.
      p. cm.
  Includes bibliographical references and index.
  ISBN 978-1-118-37458-0 (pbk.); ISBN 978-1-118-41731-7 (ebk); ISBN 978-1-118-42069-0 (ebk);
ISBN 978-1-118-43429-1 (ebk)
  1. Interpersonal communication. 2. Comprehension. 3. Explanation
(Linguistics) 4. Business communication. I. Title.
  BF637.C45L45 2013
  302.2–dc23
                                                                    2012022700

Printed in the United States of America
10 9 8 7 6 5 4 3 2 1

For Sachi

CONTENTS

Preface   *xi*

Author Note   *xv*

Introduction   *xvii*

PART 1   **Plan**   **1**

Chapter 1   Learning to Run   3

Chapter 2   What Is an Explanation?   7

What Is Not An Explanation   *8*

Defining Explanation   *9*

Explanations Require Empathy   *10*

Act and Art   *11*

Look at Your Fish   *12*

Explanation Lowers the Cost of Understanding   *13*

An Explanation Is a Way to Package Ideas   *14*

Explanations Answer the Question ''Why?''   *16*

Explanations Make People Care   *16*

Chapter 3   Why Explanations Fail   23

All About Confidence   *24*

Assumptions Cause Failure   *24*

Words Can Hurt   *26*

We Lack Understanding   *27*

We Want to Appear Smart   *28*

	The Direct Approach—No Context	*30*
	Summary	*32*
Chapter 4	Planning Your Explanations	33
	Identifying Explanation Problems	*34*
PART 2	**Package**	**43**
Chapter 5	Packaging Ideas	45
	Stepping Outside the Bubble	*46*
	What Goes into the Packaging?	*48*
Chapter 6	Context	51
	Forest then Trees	*53*
	Solving the Context Problem	*56*
	Context in Explanation—We Can All Agree	*61*
	Context and Pain	*63*
	Example: Google Docs	*63*
	On the Explanation Scale	*65*
	Summary	*66*
Chapter 7	Story	67
	Stories Versus Facts	*68*
	But I'm Not a Storyteller	*69*
	Common Craft and Stories	*71*
	The Simple Ingredient: People	*73*
	Using Stories in Explanation	*74*
	Basic Story Format	*75*
	When Does Storytelling Not *Work?*	*77*
	Personification and Story	*79*
	On the Explanation Scale	*81*
	Summary	*81*
Chapter 8	Connections	83
	Connecting Your Long Lost Uncle—Old Versus New	*84*
	Building-on Versus Establishing	*87*

Analogy   *89*
Common Craft Videos   *90*
On the Explanation Scale   *92*
Summary   *92*

Chapter 9   Description   93
Explaining Web Browsers   *95*
Explanation Is Not a Recipe   *97*
On The Explanation Scale   *99*
Summary   *99*

Chapter 10   Simplification   103

Chapter 11   Constraints   113
Common Craft and Constraints   *115*
Constraints and Your Explanations   *117*
Summary   *119*

Chapter 12   Preparing for and Writing an Explanation   121
The Common Craft Writing Process   *122*
Big Ideas   *123*
Research and Discovery   *123*
Script Writing   *125*
The Real Thing   *128*

Chapter 13   Bringing an Explanation Together   131

PART 3   **Present**   **147**

Chapter 14   Common Craft's Lessons Learned   149
Common Craft Gets Started   *149*
Ten Lessons Learned from Common Craft Explanations   *151*

Chapter 15   Right Medium for the Message   157
A Transformation   *158*
Media Options   *159*
Presentation Modes   *161*

	Recording and Distribution Options	*164*
	Constraints Come to the Rescue	*165*
	Summary	*171*
Chapter 16	Visuals	173
	You Can Use Visuals	*178*
	Dan Roam's 6 × 6 Rule	*178*
	Common Craft Visual Metaphors	*186*
	Noise and Simplicity in Visuals	*188*
	Infographics	*191*
	Creating Digital Visuals	*193*
	Summary	*193*
Chapter 17	Emma and Carlos	195
	Epilogue	*202*
Chapter 18	Explanation Culture and Your Life as an Explainer	203
	Your Life as An Explainer	*206*
Acknowledgments		*209*
Links to Common Craft Videos		*211*
About the Author		*215*
Bibliography		*217*
Index		*219*

PREFACE

Chances are that you explained something recently—why dinner tastes the way it does, why you were late for a meeting, what an article means to your company. We explain so many different things so frequently that we take the art of explanation for granted. This is a tragedy because a great explanation can make our ideas come to life, invite people to care and be motivated to learn more. However, we lose the opportunity to do this unless we recognize that explanation is an essential skill we can learn and master.

Imagine the potential that better explanations have for both your personal and professional interactions. What if your boss, accountant, team member, or mother could suddenly explain ideas in a more understandable way? What if they could put themselves in your shoes and make their ideas clear in a way that acknowledged your perspective? That is the goal of this book. I want to help you and the people around you become better explainers because we desperately need better explanations. Although this book is primarily aimed at professionals, it is meant for everyone, and intended to make the world a more understandable place in which to live and work.

The Art of Explanation is built on my years of experience in creating explanations for organizations and educators. My company, Common Craft, is known around the world for making complex ideas easy to understand in the the form of short videos. Through projects with companies such as Google, LEGO, Intel, and Ford Motor Company and the creation of our own library of video explanations, we have been students of explanation for many years. We have experimented and studied the explanation process and seen what is possible. Our videos have been viewed more than 50 million

times online, and no other brand is better known for explanations (http://commoncraft
.com/videos).

This book, however, is not a series of case studies and exercises or an academic exploration of "the science of explanation." More than anything, it is a manifesto based on our experiences as professional explainers. We believe deeply in the power of explanation and see this book as an invitation to recognize that power by looking at explanation from a new perspective. When you do, you will see that it represents an unexplored part of your communications, a skill you can understand, practice, and improve.

The various ideas, approaches, and models I provide in these pages are secondary to a simple, higher-level goal: to make explanation a priority. This means thinking about how you explain ideas and how you can put explanations to work to accomplish your goals. It requires that you use explanation as a strategy in problem solving. You must also introduce others to the idea that explanations can create positive change.

It is this overarching perspective that matters because, as the title suggests, explanation *is* an art. Although there are tools, tactics and ideas that help, we all explain differently, and that is the beauty of it. Explanations do not follow a set of specific steps and rules. They are effective because of the perspective and intent of the explainer. Looking at a problem through the lens of explanation can reveal challenges that may not have been visible before. When the intent is to create an explanation to address these challenges, we all have the potential to use the ideas in this book to build explanations in our own way.

Many of these ideas and concepts are introduced via short, fictional stories of individuals who discover the challenges and potential of explanation in various situations. These stories reflect what we believe is one of the most powerful aspects of explanation: presenting ideas from a person's or group's perspective. They also serve as an antidote to endless bullet points and lists, and provide you with an entertaining way to absorb and remember ideas.

Multiple examples of our own explanations are included, all of which have corresponding video scripts or links to videos on our website. These scripts give concrete examples of our approach to specific explanation problems that have a record of success and are a model for your own explanations.

The book is organized into three parts that align with the basic process of creating explanations—Plan, Package, and Present:

Part 1: Plan

This part of the book is meant to build a solid foundation for the idea of explanation. To create successful explanations, we need to answer such basic questions as:

- What is an explanation?
- What makes an explanation successful?
- Why do explanations fail?

The answers to these questions help us see that an explanation answers a specific kind of question—one that challenges us in many ways. We look at the factors that cause explanations to fail and where they originate.

The last chapter of this part introduces the idea of explanation problems and provides a simple model to plan and introduce explanations. We'll see how one startup company discovered an explanation problem and used the Explanation Scale to explore it and address it.

Part 2: Package

This part of the book moves from planning to production. After becoming familiar with the basics of explanations and explanation problems, we dive into ideas and strategies that can help to solve them. The big idea is to think about an explanation as a way to package ideas into a form that makes them more understandable. Elements of packaging include:

- Context
- Story

- Connections
- Descriptions

The chapters in this section introduce specific strategies and examples that present complex ideas in a way that accounts for the audience's needs. They refer to the Explanation Scale and discuss how to create "stepping stones" to better understanding. These chapters also explore concepts such as constraints and simplification as ways to approach packaging.

Part 3: Present

Explanations are not meant to sit on a shelf—they are meant to be shared. Therefore, this part will examine how we put explanations to work in organizations, and will explore the various media that can give explanations power to reach your audience.

The essential points from the first two parts are put to work here in a story about an organization that discovers the power of packaging ideas into explanations. Other chapters discuss the potential of combining explanations with a communication strategy that amplifies the impact of an explanation by making it sharable inside and outside an organization. We close the book with a forward-looking chapter entitled "Your Life as an Explainer" that describes real world examples to show how explanation skills can benefit your company, career, and even your profession.

The Art of Explanation is for anyone who wants their ideas, products, and services to be easy to understand. However, it is more than that; it is a *perspective*. If we can improve explanations even a little, the positive potential for ourselves, our organizations, and the people around us could be tremendous. I invite you to take the first step.

AUTHOR NOTE

Using QR Codes with your Smartphone

Throughout this book, I reference a number of short Common Craft videos. The videos are on our website and can be viewed for free with most smartphones.

To access the videos quickly, we've provided QR (Quick Response) codes. These codes are like links on a website, but instead of clicking them, you point your camera phone at them and use an app to scan the code, which opens the corresponding web page on your device. This makes it quick and easy to watch as you read without typing long URLs.

To use QR codes, you need a smartphone and a free app. Search your device's app store for "QR Reader" and download it. Then open the app and follow the instructions to scan a QR code.

You can test this process using the code above. Once the code has been scanned, select "Go to URL" (or something similar) and the web page will appear. Just click "play" to watch QR Codes Explained by Common Craft.

To see a complete list of the Common Craft videos referenced in the book and their URLs, see the Links to Common Craft Videos section at the end of this book.

INTRODUCTION

For most of my life (especially in school), I struggled to grasp some of the subjects I was supposed to be learning. Although I grasped subjects such as science and history fairly easily, topics such as math and accounting consistently proved to be challenging. In my mind, these subjects were made up of thousands of rules that I had to memorize to solve the associated problems. The ideas seemed to float around in my head without any foundation or place.

As so many students who struggle do, I felt inadequate at the time, as if my brain was not wired for solving these problems. I became a person who said "I'm not good at math" and avoided anything related to it. The notion of trying to memorize rule after rule frustrated me, and I wondered how others did it with such apparent ease. Were they simply more skilled at memorization? What was I missing?

At the same time, however, I knew I was a capable student. Along with science and history, writing came easily to me. But as much as I wanted math and subjects like it to work for me, it seemed like the light bulb never went on.

However, I learned to work with this apparent limitation throughout my years of education. I eventually earned a graduate degree in health administration and moved to Seattle, where I currently live. It was during this phase of my career that I identified the underlying cause of my struggle with subjects like math and started to see how the same problem affected others. When I looked back, it seemed like there were some people in my classes who could look at a set of rules or details and naturally see the big picture—in other words, the *why*. They seemed to be able to understand math and accounting at a higher level, whereas students like me were getting so mired in trying to memorize the *how* that the *why* faded into the background. We could still pass tests and make good grades, but we did it by memorizing facts, not by developing a true understanding of the material.

The more I thought about this, the clearer the solution became. My learning style meant that I needed a way to approach new ideas in a unique way. I needed to see the big picture first, the foundation of the details. Therefore, to understand accounting, I needed to understand business basics first. To understand math, I needed to understand the reasoning behind it first. I needed to see the *forest* before the *trees*.

Soon enough I realized what was missing: I needed better explanations. My learning style demanded that I see the *why* before the *how*. This revelation became a part of my communication style. I became a student of communication and watched my friends and peers explain ideas. I began to recognize how people got confused or lost confidence in their ability to understand something completely. This experience made a deep impression on me.

But it was not until I got involved in the technology industry in 1998 that this realization became a part of my work. I was hired as a data analyst at a healthcare software company in Bellevue, Washington. Within two years I met my wife and business partner, Sachi, and I developed a strong passion for the idea that customers should be able to communicate and get support using message boards on the company website. What is now known as social media was called *online communities* in 1999, and I wanted to be the online community manager.

As you might imagine, this was not an easy sell inside the company. Most of my colleagues had never considered the potential of an online community and were naturally risk-averse. But I had a plan: I would explain my way into creating this program. So I set up meetings with product managers and created materials that supported my ideas. I educated my colleagues in the way *I* had wanted to be educated throughout my life.

I provided a foundation by building context and discussing big ideas—the forest. I helped them feel confident that they fully understood what I wanted to do before talking about any details—the trees. I planned my explanations and told stories that highlighted how this online community had the potential to be a rich source of customer information. It could even become an early warning system for product teams.

I asked them to imagine a world in which customers could solve each other's problems. I explained the idea to executives and connected it to the company's strategy and goals. Slowly but surely, the stakeholders saw the potential, and most became advocates.

Soon enough I was the online community manager—a job I held until 2003, when I left to found Common Craft. I launched it as an online community consulting company aimed at helping organizations understand and implement their own online communities. My job as an explainer was just beginning.

My role as a consultant was to influence my clients and help them see and understand new opportunities. I soon realized my clients were experiencing difficulties very similar to those I experienced when attempting to understand certain subjects in school. Their view of social media was like my view of accounting: they knew the words and had memorized the features of various tools, but they had no foundation. They were stuck with countless trees, but no forest, and like me, they could not fully apply what they were learning.

This gave me an idea.

I decided to take subjects such as wikis and RSS feeds—topics that had proved challenging for my clients to grasp—and write my own explanations using the tagline "in plain English." The idea was to help solve a problem for my clients and to create something interesting for the Common Craft blog. This was the first time I realized that my unique perspective on explanation could be a useful business tool. I had developed the ability to put myself in other people's shoes and create media that helped them feel confident. They loved reading the blog posts and I enjoyed writing them, but it would be a few years before they would be called into action.

At around the same time, I put my explanation skills to the test. A few companies sponsored what they called "The Perfect Corporate Weblog Pitch Contest." The idea was to explain the value of corporate weblogs in the time it takes to ride an elevator (under 160 words). When I saw this contest, I thought to myself, "Man, I am all over this!" It was true. My award-winning pitch read as follows:

First, think about the value of the Wall Street Journal *to business leaders. The value it provides is context—the* Journal *allows readers to see themselves in the context of the financial world each day, which enables more informed decision making.*

With this in mind, think about your company as a microcosm of the financial world. Can your employees see themselves in the context of the whole company? Would more informed decisions be made if employees and leaders had access to internal news sources? Weblogs serve this need. By making internal websites simple to update, weblogs allow individuals and teams to maintain online journals that chronicle projects inside the company. These professional journals make it easy to produce and access internal news, providing context to the company—context that can profoundly affect decision making. In this way, weblogs allow employees and leaders to make more informed decisions through increasing their awareness of internal news and events.

My goal was to convey the value of weblogs in a way that would appeal to the judges; however, I learned something else from this experience. For the first time, I felt that explanation was not simply a tactic or way of approaching communication. It was something that excited and motivated me. I specifically remember my heart beating rapidly when I drafted the corporate weblog pitch. It made me feel like I had found my calling, like I was born to make ideas easier for others to understand in the form of explanations.

I came to realize over the next few years that the consulting clients with whom I worked were not unique in their thoughts about technology. The general public also struggled to see the value of these new online products and tools. Most people were constantly caught up in the features and details. They wanted to stay ahead of the curve but were cautious about wasting time on a product they did not fully understand.

The tragedy from my perspective was that the tools were often free, easy to use, and could have a positive impact on people's lives. However, people weren't adopting them because of how they were *explained*. The technologists were doing the explaining, and doing it poorly.

We came to call this an *explanation problem*, which is when the biggest barrier to adoption is not design, features, or benefits but communication. And the problem was epidemic. Thousands of life changing tools and ideas were not being used because they lacked clear explanations of their value.

When Sachi joined me at Common Craft in 2006, we set out to solve this problem. It was the year YouTube went mainstream; suddenly, anyone could easily publish videos to the Web. We started to experiment and looked for ways to make video part of Common Craft. After feeling awkward trying to be the guy standing in front of a whiteboard, Sachi had the idea to point a camera straight down onto a whiteboard and use hands, markers, and paper cut-outs to tell a story.

Common Craft videos were born in 2007, and we created our first video based on a blog post for my clients from years before, entitled "RSS in Plain English" (www.commoncraft.com/video/rss). We shot the video in our basement with no expectations or video production skills, and it showed. We lit the whiteboard with the strongest portable lights we had: bedroom lamps. And for the narration, I spoke directly into the microphone on the camera. As it turned out, this three-minute video changed our lives.

Sachi with our second generation studio setup, summer 2007.

We posted it on YouTube in April, and it became a viral hit. It was viewed tens of thousands of times the first day and we received a torrent of e-mails, comments, and blog posts about our work. People contacted us and encouraged us to make more videos. It was one of the most exciting days of my life. Our explanation was a hit because it solved the RSS explanation problem and invited people to use it by helping them see it from a new, more understandable perspective.

The next question became: can we do it again? We published our second video about a month later, which was also based on a previous blog post. This one was called "Wikis in Plain English" (www.commoncraft.com/video/wikis), and was received in a similar way. People seemed to love our videos and want more.

By the end of the summer of 2007, we had published four more videos and started making custom videos for products and services. In August of 2007, we decided that Common Craft would become a video production company that specialized in video explanations. We redesigned our website, and our tagline became "Our Product Is Explanation." One of our first custom videos, called "Google Docs in Plain English," hit the web that fall (www.commoncraft.com/google-docs-plain-english). We were on our way.

Since that time, people around the world have come to know Common Craft for our explanation skills. We have made more than 100 video explanations in the same format as the first video on RSS—what is now known as Common Craft Style. Our videos have been viewed more than 50 million times online and we have worked with companies such as LEGO, Intel, Google, Dropbox, and Microsoft to explain their products and services. Further, teachers and students are now creating their own video explanations in classrooms and calling them "Common Craft Style Videos." Perhaps no company is better known for video explanations than Common Craft.

Now more than ever, I am a believer in the power of explanation, and not just for product and service videos. I believe it is a skill that everyone can learn and improve upon, and one that is needed to help people grasp ideas in a useful and productive way. This book is designed to give everyone an opportunity to rethink how he or she explains ideas, and learn to package them into explanations that work.

the **art** of **explanation**

PART 1

Plan

CHAPTER 1

Learning to Run

 Trevor limped through the front door, sore again. These past few months had been tough on his joints. Six months ago he picked up running again after his doctor said he needed to get more exercise. To help keep himself motivated, he set a goal of completing a half-marathon within a year. But it didn't seem like this was going to happen—not the way things were looking now. Trevor was beginning to realize that his body just couldn't take a beating these days, and he joked with friends that he felt like an old man at 45.

It wasn't always this way. Trevor had always been a runner in one way or another. He played soccer in high school, and started to run as a way to stay in shape in college. He took to it naturally. But as he moved onto a career, his time became limited and he ran less and less frequently.

Trevor knew that something needed to change if he was going to complete the half-marathon. He tried a variety of tactics—buying new running shoes, wearing knee braces, and concentrating on stretching. However, nothing seemed to work, and the date for the half-marathon was drawing closer.

Trevor had recently been enjoying a drink with a friend and mentioned that he was having a difficult time preparing for the race. After some probing, his friend asked a simple question that he wasn't sure how to answer: "Have you tried changing how you run?" Perplexed, Trevor replied, "I'm not sure what you mean . . . I run how I run. It's always been the same—one foot in front of the other!" After a chuckle, his friend asked again "Seriously, have you ever thought about *how you run*—and what you could do to run *better*?"

The thought had never occurred to Trevor. He had always taken his running style for granted. After all, it had usually come easily to him, and he achieved the results he wanted. He assumed that his running style was as good as it ever could be, so he responded "Nah, the way I run is fine. And anyway, aren't we born with the ability to run?"

His friend replied, "Of course we can all run. But like anything, there is an art and skill to running, and part of getting what you want out of it is knowing how to run correctly."

Trevor had never considered that there might be a right or wrong way to run, and questioned incredulously, "What could possibly make my running better?"

His friend smiled and answered, "Look it up." And that is just what he did.

Trevor's perspective started to change within a few days. The more he researched, the more he saw running as a skill that he could improve. He learned about proper posture, stride, and how a foot strikes the surface, and discovered tactics that professional runners use to stay healthy. For the first time, he could see that his joint problems were likely due to *how* he was running. A feeling of relief came over him. Unlike his age, *this* was something he could change!

As he trained for the race, he began paying attention to his form and movements. Within a few weeks, his knee and back pain began to fade, and his endurance seemed to jump, which gave him the energy to run longer than ever. The half-marathon now seemed like a reality and it felt good.

If you ask Trevor about running today, he will tell you that his only regret is not discovering how he could improve his running earlier. But now that he has this new perspective, a full marathon doesn't seem too far away.

Like Trevor and his running, we all take *explanation* for granted. Because it is a natural part of how we communicate, the thought may never occur to us that explanation is a skill we can improve and put to work in achieving our goals. In this way, running and explanation have much in common:

- We have the ability to do it
- We may do it so frequently that we never think about it
- We think the way in which we do it is normal
- We never consider that we could improve the way we do it, but,
- Improvement *is* possible, and creates positive results

Because explanation is a skill that we can improve and apply to nearly every part of our lives, let's get started in doing so. In Chapter 2 we'll define *explanation* and consider the characteristics that make it useful and powerful.

What Is an Explanation?

For most of my life, I never considered the definition of the word "explanation"—and I doubt I am alone in this. We all explain things so often, why would we need to define something we do every day?

The fact is, however, that most of us take explanation for granted. For many people, it's just something that happens. Someone asks a question, we answer it in the form of an explanation. We do not often step back and think about what makes an explanation an explanation or how we could approach it differently. Our explanations happen without much planning or editing.

It's a little like dancing. Your grace on the dance floor may mean that you take dancing for granted: it just happens when there is a rhythm. But even the best dancer can only get so far without defining specific dances, such as what makes the samba the samba and the waltz the waltz. These definitions create a standard form and shape that can be honed and refined. Only by defining the standards of the dance can we hope to improve it.

We'll begin to define explanation below by first looking at what is NOT an explanation. This will allow us to see it not as a simple shake of the hips, but as a dance that has a deliberate form, intent, and emotion.

What Is *Not* An Explanation

The following is a list of the various ways we can relate ideas and information. Although we will define explanation a bit later, it is useful to think about what is *not* an explanation. For instance, if explanation is the samba, these are some other dances:

Description—A description is a direct account of an action, person, event, and so on in which the intent is to help someone imagine something through words. For example, if I describe my coffee mug, my intent is to provide details that help you picture it. A description may relate that a mug is white, four inches tall, has a single curved handle, and is made of ceramic.

Definition—A definition is a description of the precise and literal meaning of something. A definition is meant to make clear exactly what something means. If I define a word, I am providing statements that help you see the exact meaning of the word. I might define coffee as a beverage that is made from roasted and ground seeds of the coffee plant.

Instruction—An instruction is a direction or order to do something. The intent of instruction is to make clear what is expected and how to proceed. If I give you instructions on how to make coffee, I am laying out the exact process or sequence of events that are required to achieve the desired outcome. Instructions may be related in short sentences such as: Insert filter into coffee maker. Pour ground coffee into filter. Pour water into coffee maker reservoir. Press start.

Elaboration—An elaboration is a presentation of information with detail, with the intent to provide a comprehensive and rigorous look at a concept, idea, theory, and so on. If I elaborate on the core concepts of coffee production, I will try to cover every detail. If I elaborate on the farming of coffee, I may describe the specific content of the soil in which it is grown, how to test the soil, and what levels of nitrogen will produce the best product for a specific geographic region.

Report—A report is a spoken or written account of an event and is intended to relay facts and details to others. If I visit coffee plantations in Colombia, I will report my experiences upon my return. This may appear in the form of a news story or magazine article and relate an account such as: "The moment I arrived at the plantation, I was offered a sample of their finest product, which I drank with joy. The company roasted the beans just a mile away, and you could smell the roasting beans in the air."

Illustration—An illustration is an example that serves to clarify an idea. The intent of an illustration is to help make an idea more real by providing an example. I might say that the size of the plantation is an illustration of the coffee company's power in the region.

Of course, this doesn't mean that these communication forms have no role in explanation. Quite the opposite, in fact; they could all contribute to improved explanations. I list them simply to show that explanation is one of many communication forms, each with its own definition. Now we can look specifically at the definition of explanation.

Defining Explanation

Let us start with a formal definition. *Explanation*, according to Merriam-Webster, is "the act or process of explaining."

OK, so maybe that's not very helpful. We obviously need to use a slightly different word. Here is the Merriam-Webster definition of *explain* as a verb: "To make known; to make plain or understandable."

We can deduce from this that an explanation is an *act or process* that makes something *known, plain,* or *understandable.* That is pretty simple and straightforward. Personally, I am fond of the current Wikipedia version (Wikipedia, 2012):

> *An explanation is a set of statements constructed to describe a set of facts which clarifies the causes, context and consequences of those facts.*

To put it into the form we used above:

Explanation—An explanation describes facts in a way that makes them understandable. The intent of an explanation is to increase understanding. If I explain coffee roasting, I am clarifying the facts and making the ideas more understandable. For example, an explanation may highlight the role of heat in giving coffee a distinctive color and flavor when roasted.

As you can see, explanation is different from the other examples above, especially in intent. Explanations make facts more understandable. It seems to be that simple, but is it? As we'll see below, there are a number of nuances and ideas that make explanations a particularly potent form of communication.

Explanations Require Empathy

Every once in a while, I encounter someone who is a natural explainer, whose approach to communication naturally jibes with many of the points illustrated here. These people seek out unique and helpful ways to explain ideas to others. Sometimes, the best are teachers and journalists who combine their natural communication style with a focus on the professional standards of their profession. When I meet one of these people, I look for common traits and ask: what do great explainers have in common?

In a word, it is *empathy*. Great explainers have the ability to picture themselves in another person's shoes and communicate from that perspective. A great example of this is offering driving directions. From my unscientific research, natural explainers are better than average at giving directions. Why? My guess is that they can account for the experience of approaching a location for the first time. They are able to block out what is already familiar to them and instead focus on what the driver is likely to see at each turn.

And so it is with explanation. Creating a great explanation involves stepping out of your own shoes and into the audience's. It is a process built on empathy, on being able to understand and share the feelings of another. Only by seeing the world through the windshield of a driver in a foreign land can we ever hope to help them feel at home.

Act and Art

We live in a world of facts and fact-makers. Scientists, for example, have very rigorous standards used when claiming a statement is a fact. As such, the scientific method is a standard process that can lead to the discovery of facts. In this way, fact-making is a science, and we are all better off for it.

But facts are not perfect. Although they may be proven many times over, they are often difficult to understand and apply. And when people provide them without much context and with a high degree of specificity, their value becomes limited. It is more difficult to make sense of facts alone, which is why we need explanations. Explanations make facts more understandable, and the need for explanations becomes clear once you think about how many important facts are out there. Imagine a world where every fact was presented as an explanation—complete with context and simple language—with the goal of making the fact understandable. We could feel confident about so much more of the world around us!

Unfortunately, this is not the case. Good, effective explanations are in short supply, for valid reasons. You might look at it as means of production. Look at science, for instance, where the scientific method can be used by anyone to validate or invalidate an idea with certainty. A particular scientist's personality, preferences, or experiences do not impact the production process; only cold hard science matters, and that opens the means of production to anyone with an interest.

Explanation of those facts, on the other hand, is more of an art. Great explanations often do not come from rigorous research and testing; they come from someone's unique approach to communication. Two people could have profoundly different ways of explaining a single idea and still achieve equal levels of understanding. Like any art form, explanation thrives on being unique and novel; it succeeds when it helps people see ideas from a new perspective. It is a conscious act that depends on creativity more than a specific formula or set of steps.

However, I do not mean to make the case that you must have a creative mind to create great explanations. My wife Sachi is a perfect example of how this is in fact *not* the case. She is very analytical and prefers a spreadsheet to a paintbrush. Although she identifies herself as not having a very creative mind, she is very good at explanation because she approaches it with the right perspective. The art of explanation is unlike the ability to draw or write poetry; it is more about perspective, or orienting yourself around the idea that explanations are creations, made of facts, that represent a new way of approaching an idea.

This is the perspective that has driven our work at Common Craft. We do not produce facts; rather, we package them. We take these facts and transform them into something that makes people feel confident and informed. And that is one of the underlying lessons of this book—that explanation is a creative act that turns facts into useful, informative, and memorable ideas.

Look at Your Fish

Although there is no formula that stamps out cookie-cutter explanations, we believe that the ability to learn the skill of explanation is all about perspective.

The challenge is to take ideas that are in plain sight and transform them into something more useful. I recently read an interview with author David McCullough that frames this idea in terms of "seeing" what is in front of everyone. The interviewer asks about a motto that McCullough has hanging framed over his desk. His answer (The Paris Review, 2012):

It says, "Look at your fish." It's the test that nineteenth-century Harvard naturalist Louis Agassiz gave every new student. He would take an odorous old fish out of a jar, set it in a tin pan in front of the student and say, Look at your fish. Then Agassiz would leave. When he came back, he would ask the student what he'd seen. Not very much, they would most often say, and Agassiz would say it again: Look at your fish. This could go on for days. The student would be encouraged to draw the fish but could use no tools for the examination, just hands and eyes. Samuel Scudder, who later became a famous entomologist and expert on grasshoppers, left us the best account of the "ordeal with the fish." After several days, he still could not see whatever it was Agassiz wanted him to see. But, he said, I see how little I saw before. Then Scudder had a brainstorm and he announced it to Agassiz the next morning: paired organs, the same on both sides. Of course! Of course! Agassiz said, very pleased. So Scudder naturally asked what he should do next, and Agassiz said, Look at your fish.

I love that story and have used it often when teaching classes on writing, because seeing is so important in this work. Insight comes, more often than not, from looking at what's been on the table all along, in front of everybody, rather than from discovering something new. Seeing is as much the job of an historian as it is of a poet or a painter, it seems to me. That's Dickens's great admonition to all writers, "Make me see."

"Make me see"—perhaps the best thing we can hope to accomplish from an explanation. If only it were as easy as looking at a fish.

Explanation Lowers the Cost of Understanding

Feeling informed is a constant struggle. Every day, headlines introduce us to new crises, discoveries, and products. Although overwhelming, most people have learned to cope by filtering out the things that do not interest them. Occasionally, interesting topics emerge that just seem too big to tackle. Examples include news about the Large Hadron Collider in Europe or recent discoveries in health-care. The cost of understanding these subjects is too high to justify the investment; it would take too much time and effort, so we filter it out.

Explanation is a powerful asset in a world of constant change; because it can lower the cost of understanding, it invites people to participate in a variety of new topics.

A good example is the story of NYU journalism professor Jay Rosen and his path to learning about the mortgage crisis in 2008. As the crisis began, we received many suggestions from our fans to explain the mortgage crisis. They were anxious about it and had no resources that helped them understand it fully. For them, the cost of figuring out all the moving parts was high—too high. They needed an explanation.

Over that summer, Ira Glass, Adam Davidson, and Alex Blumberg set out to solve this problem and produced an episode of the *This American Life* radio show whose goal was to explain the crisis. Called "The Giant Pool of Money," it is an amazing example of explanation at work (*This American Life*, 2008).

One of the listeners to the show was Jay Rosen. From his blog (PressThink, 2008):

Going into the program, I didn't understand the mortgage mess one bit: subprime loans were ruining Wall Street firms? And I care because they are old, respected firms?

That's what I knew.

Coming out of the program, I understood the complete scam: what happened, why it happened, and why I should care. I had a good sense of the motivations and situations of players all down the line. Civic mastery was mine over a complex story, dense with technical terms, unfolding on many fronts and different levels, with no heroes. And the villains were mostly abstractions!

The hour-long show successfully lowered the cost of understanding a very complex issue for Jay and countless others. And although that is a wonderful outcome, it's only part of the equation. Rosen continues:

I noticed something in the weeks after I first listened to "The Giant Pool of Money." I became a customer for ongoing news about the mortgage mess and the credit crisis that developed from it (since the program's conclusion explained how one caused the other.) 'Twas a successful act of explanation that put me in the market for information. Before that moment, I had ignored hundreds of news reports about Americans losing their homes, the housing market crashing, banks in trouble, Wall Street firms on the brink of collapse.

"'Twas a successful act of explanation that put me in the market for information." What a powerful statement! The explanation moved him from being someone who simply filtered out mortgage crisis information to someone who actively sought it out. For the first time, Rosen knew enough to care.

We all feel indifference at one point towards some topic. There are simply not enough hours in the day to figure it *all* out. Thankfully, we have explanations, which lower the cost of figuring out an idea and invite people to become customers of it in the future.

An Explanation Is a Way to Package Ideas

The art of explanation is the art of transforming facts into a more understandable package. Chances are you know the facts of plagiarism: the act of passing someone else's work off as your own, or using someone's ideas without credit. The facts—and the consequences—are clear in this case. Although it is not often an illegal act, it is serious enough for people to lose jobs and be kicked out of school.

And the facts are also quite clear for students in high school and college. They know that plagiarism is wrong and has serious consequences. Despite this clarity, however, it is still a big problem for schools—so much so that Common Craft received multiple requests to make a video that explains plagiarism. In 2011, we decided to make this video and started "looking at our fish." This meant thinking about how we could package the facts about plagiarism into a form that would help students see it from a new perspective.

This process of packaging was creative; we weren't simply making the language simpler to understand. Rather, we had to think about context and themes that *live in the same world* as plagiarism. Over time we started to see that plagiarism is often presented in terms of facts, that is, "it is against the rules." But the idea behind what makes plagiarism wrong goes much deeper. It threatens a system on which we all depend. Plagiarism is not just cheating; it actually reduces our ability to keep track of who made contributions to the knowledge we need to be successful. It is disrespectful to our entire system of ideas.

It was this perspective that drove our thinking on how to explain plagiarism. Here is the transcript from the first 42 seconds of the 2:41 length video:

You have something in common with the smartest people in the world. You see, everyone has ideas. We use our minds to create something original, whether it's a poem, a drawing, a song, or a scientific paper.

Some of the most important ideas are published and make it into books, journals, newspapers, and trustworthy websites that become the building blocks for things we all learn.

But ideas are also very personal, and we need dependable ways to keep track of the people behind the ideas we use because they deserve credit for their contribution, just as you do if someone uses your idea. Passing off another person's ideas or words as your own, without credit, is called *plagiarism*. Whether it's your friend's term paper or words of a well-known author, plagiarism is cheating and dishonest.

Notice that this explanation did not even mention plagiarism until the very end of the section, about a third of the way through the video. This was our approach to packaging plagiarism into a form that discusses facts, but presents them in a way that is unique.

Explanations Answer the Question "Why?"

It is really quite breathtaking how much of the world around us is based in fact. There is a reason for almost everything. Consider the laws of physics. Through years of research and experiments, scientists have theorized, with very high confidence, the basic rules of our universe. We can be certain at what temperature water boils and freezes at sea level. We know the exact speed of sound and how to calculate how much weight a wall can bear.

In essence, science has helped us make sense of the world by showing that there is a *reason* things are the way they are. There is a reason that water freezes at 32 degrees Fahrenheit and airplanes can fly. The laws of our universe have been tested and are proven: they explain *why*.

Unfortunately, many of the facts and ideas we see on a day-to-day basis cannot be defined by laws of the universe. We cannot, for example, explain Twitter's popularity in terms of gravity or inertia. We need explanations to tell us why Twitter is so popular, or to illustrate why it makes sense to save for retirement. Explanation is the art of not just packaging facts but presenting them in a way that answers the question "why?"—as in, why does it make sense to do this? Or why should I care?

Explanation is not focused on facts, laws, or specifics. Explanation is the art of showing *why* the facts, laws, and specifics make sense. By clarifying the reason an idea makes sense, we can put the facts into perspective. As such, explanation is the practice of packaging facts into a form that makes them easier to understand and apply.

Explanations Make People Care

A quick search on Google about how to do something will reveal a plethora of information. From plucking a chicken to changing a tire to programming a mobile app, how-to instructional texts, photos, and videos are arguably some of the most informative and powerful features of the Web. Most instructions are tactical, a step-by-step process that, when followed, achieves the desired outcome.

You could say that this information is a type of explanation. And although that's a valid point, there's actually a better way to think about what explanations really are.

Let's return to our earlier points. First, explanations are packages of ideas that help people see what is already in front of them in a new way. Second, explanations show why things are the way they are. These are not what people consider when they're assembling Ikea furniture or mixing a cocktail.

Explanations have a different goal: to present an idea in a way that makes people *care*. Explanations grab their attention and let them see an idea from a personal perspective so they can make informed decisions about learning more. And that is the key point: explanations are packages of ideas that help people feel confident in choosing to learn more because they *care* about the idea.

Twitter is a great example. Twitter is a free service that makes it easy for people to share short updates with other individuals who choose to "follow" them. I joined Twitter in November of 2006 and quickly became addicted. It was clear that Twitter was going to be important, but it was also clear the service had a big challenge to face: it was a fundamentally new idea that was difficult to explain. The facts concerning Twitter are fairly simple: you post updates about what's going on in your life and read updates from others. The problem is that the facts did a poor job of presenting the value of engaging in these kinds of online interactions. Most people who heard about Twitter for the first time had essentially the same reaction: "Why would I want to do *that*?" It was only after experiencing it that they could see the value of it. The experience made them care in a way that the facts could not.

This became a challenge for Common Craft. How could we explain Twitter in a way that makes people care enough to want to try it? Is it possible to make a three-minute video that packages the ideas behind Twitter in a form that helps people see them in a new way?

In 2007, we created "Twitter in Plain English" as a way to explain the service to all those who asked, "Why would I want to do *that*?" As the final cuts of the video came together, I contacted Twitter co-founder Biz Stone, who loved it. We made a handshake deal, and within a few weeks the video appeared on the front page of Twitter.com, where it remained for more than a year. Since that time, the video has been viewed about 15 million times and has turned innumerable people onto the service. The main reason I think it was successful is that it helped people see why they should care about Twitter.

Here is the transcript:

So, what are you doing? It's one of the first questions we often ask friends and family. Even if the answer is just mowing the lawn or cooking dinner, it's interesting to us. It makes us feel connected and a part of each other's lives.

Unfortunately, most of our day-to-day lives are hidden from people that care. Booooo! Of course, we have e-mail and blogs and phones to keep us connected, but you wouldn't send an e-mail to tell a friend you're having coffee—your friend doesn't need to know that.

But—what about people that want to know about the little things that happen in your life? Real life happens between blog posts and e-mails and now there's a way to share.

This is Twitter in Plain English

Thanks to Twitter, it's possible to share short, bite-sized updates about your life and follow the updates of people that matter to you via the web. Yaay! Here's how it works.

Meet Carla. She's addicted to her mobile phone, reads blogs every day and has contacts all over the world. She heard about Twitter and was skeptical—she's already overloaded with information. After some of her friends couldn't stop talking about it, she gave it a try.

She signed up for free and saw that Twitter pages look a little like blogs with very short posts. Each page is personal and has updates from friends.

She got started by looking up her friends on Twitter.com. After finding a few, she clicked "follow" to start seeing their updates on her Twitter page. Within hours, she began to see a different side of people she chose to follow.

She didn't know that Steven in Seattle was a baseball fan, or that Julia in London was reading a new investment book. The little messages from Twitter painted a picture of her friends, family, and co-workers that she'd never seen before—it was the real world.

Soon she became a fan of Twitter and posted updates every day. Her friends followed her updates and learned that she recently discovered a passion for Van Halen. They could see Carla's life between blog posts and e-mails.

For Carla, Twitter worked because it was simple. The updates were always short—under 140 characters each. Plus, she could post updates and follow her friends using the Twitter website, software on her browser, a mobile phone, or instant messages. She wasn't tied to one device.

By asking members to answer the question "what are you doing?" Carla found that Twitter brought her closer to people that matter to her—140 characters at a time.

Find out what your friends are doing at Twitter.com.

By focusing on making people care about Twitter, we were able to help them see value and finally understand why Twitter is popular.

Explanations that make people care also have another benefit: people who care about an idea are often *more motivated to learn more*. That's what happened to Jay Rosen when an explanation prompted him to become a customer of news about the mortgage crisis. For example, think about how intimidating it is to start learning to program software. At first, it looks like an impossibly complex challenge; someone has to believe it is worth the time and effort to get through it. They must *care*. This is the case with almost any challenge. Caring is the first step: if an explanation can help that person start to care, the rest is much easier.

EXPLANATION AT WORK: TANIA LOMBROZO, COGNITIVE SCIENTIST

In researching this book, I began to wonder about the academic side of explanation and what I could learn from researchers in the fields of psychology and philosophy. Although some theories go back as far Aristotle, more modern research attempts to show the structure and function of explanation. Like almost any academic research, the study of explanation is often presented through studies and research papers, a review of which I've cited in the following. It is a very broad field of study and one that applies across disciplines. It's important to note that I'm providing the information below for reference. It represents a different, more science-based approach to thinking about explanation; however, it's one that, in most cases, matches our own experience as explainers.

(continued)

(*continued*)

Tania Lombrozo, PhD., is a cognitive psychologist and assistant professor of psychology at the University of California, Berkeley, where she directs the concepts and cognition lab. I spoke with her about her work on explanation, and she directed me to a review paper she wrote that brings together much of the current research.

Before diving in, I want to point out that Dr. Lombrozo made it clear that the study of explanation has yet to provide widely accepted definitions of what represents an explanation, or what makes one successful. This was both heartening and disappointing to hear. As an author of a book about explanation, an academic definition would be quite helpful. But at the same time, this lack of an academic definition goes to the heart of what makes an explanation an art versus a science. My hope is that this lack of definition may represent an opportunity to contribute my own perspective to the discussion.

Dr. Lombrozo's paper, titled "Explanation and Abductive Inference," appeared in the *Oxford Handbook of Thinking and Reasoning*.* It outlines a review of current thinking about explanation. A few big points from the paper follow:

A first step toward precision, if not definition, is to distinguish explanation as a product *from explanation as a* process *(see also Chin-Parker & Bradner, 2010). As a product, an explanation is a proposition or judgment, typically linguistic, that addresses an explicit or implicit request for an explanation. As a process, explanation is a cognitive activity that aims to generate one or more explanation "products" but need not succeed in order to be engaged.*

In simple terms, we can view explanation as two different things: something you think about *(process)* and something that's shared *(product)*. In terms of functions, we see that explanations can help us deal with how we understand and adapt to a changing environment. Dr. Lombrozo continues:

While many plausible functions for explanation have been proposed, both philosophers and psychologists have emphasized that explanations could be valuable because they scaffold the kind of learning that supports adaptive behavior. For example, Craik (1943) described explanation as "a kind of distance-receptor in time, which enables organisms to adapt themselves to situations that are about to arise." Heider (1958) suggested that we explain events in order to relate them to more general processes, allowing us

*Tania Lombrozo. "Explanation and Abductive Inference," in *The Oxford Handbook of Thinking and Reasoning*, ed. Keith J. Holyoak, PhD, and Robert G. Morrison, PhD (2012); 530 words, 260–276.

''to attain a stable environment and have the possibility of controlling it.'' In other words, explanations put us in a better position to predict and control the future. Gopnik (2000) provocatively compares explanation to orgasm, suggesting that the phenomenological satisfaction of explanation is our evolutionarily provided incentive to engage in theory formation, as orgasm is to reproduction.

Explanation as orgasm and way to predict and control the future—I can't think of a more compelling way to look at it.

Explanation and Learning

This is a subject near and dear to our hearts, as our work has always been based on explanation as a learning tool. We see the potential for teachers and professionals of all types to include explanations as a specific part of their teaching. In most cases, this means showing a video explanation at the beginning of a training session to get everyone on the same page. As Dr. Lombrozo states:

Given the intimate relationship between explanation and understanding, it is no surprise that explanation has a profound impact in learning. There are at least three ways in which explanation can influence learning. First, there is the matter of which explanations are sought, which constrains what one learns about the environment. For example, upon first encountering an elephant you're likely to wonder why it has a trunk, but less likely to wonder why the number of its legs is a perfect square. Second, processes involved in the evaluation of explanations can influence what is learned from provided explanations, be it in educational or everyday situations. And third, the very process of generating explanations, be it for oneself or others, can influence one's own understanding and ability to generalize to novel contexts.

The third point really hits home for two reasons: First, I see evidence of it every time we make a Common Craft video. Ideas that seem disconnected at first often come together while writing a script for a video. My own understanding of the subject increases by working on the explanation. Second, more teachers have adopted ''Common Craft Style'' videos as classroom exercises. Often, the class is divided into groups and directed to create their own explanations of subjects such as world history, biology, and political science. They then film these explanations with paper cutouts, creating an experience like a Common Craft video. Dr. Lombrozo's research supports the

(continued)

(continued)

feedback we've heard from teachers that this exercise of generating explanations brings subjects to life for the students:

Perhaps surprisingly, generating explanations can be a more effective mechanism for learning than receiving explanation. This phenomenon has been demonstrated in the context of peer tutoring, where tutors often profit more than tutees (e.g., Hooper, 1992; Roscoe & Chi, 2008; Ross & Cousins, 1995). The learning benefit of engaging in explanation — be it to oneself or to others — is known as the self-explanation effect (Chi, Bassok, Lewis, Reimann, & Glaser, 1989; Chi, de Leeuw, Chiu, & LaVancher, 1994), and has been found for preschoolers through adults, for a range of educational materials, and for both declarative and procedural knowledge (for review, see Fonseca & Chi, 2010). In a typical experiment, one group of participants is prompted to explain to themselves as they study an expository text or worked examples, such as math problems. These participants are compared with those in one or more control groups who study the same material without the prompt to explain, often with an alternative task (e.g., thinking aloud) or matched for study time. The typical finding is that participants who explain outperform their nonexplaining peers on a posttest, with the greatest benefit for transfer problems that require going beyond the material presented.

Bottom line: The act of explaining helps us understand an idea more completely, a concept that's important to keep in mind when reading the rest of this book. Our focus throughout is the audience and how we can help them feel confident when learning a new idea. Although this is the priority, it's also helpful to remember that we, the explainers, achieve a positive side effect at the same time: we increase our own understanding of the subject.

It seems to me that this represents another kind of opportunity. If, having read this book, you are in a position to help others with explanations, you might find that asking them to create an explanation produces a product. However, it does even more than that; it helps them see the idea from a new, more informed perspective.

CHAPTER 3

Why Explanations Fail

 Blank stares: you've seen them before. Usually after you've spent the previous 10 minutes trying to make your audience, however small or large, as excited as you are about your idea. But it's clear from the looks on their faces that they did not get it. And when this happens, there's no way to move forward without leaving people behind.

I've been there. When I was a consultant, I prided myself on being able to explain technology, but I failed a number of times. My passion and interest caused me to speak quickly and skip important points. I sometimes assumed people were following along until I saw on their faces that they did not get the point.

Every day, many companies, homes, and schools are filled with blank stares and discouraged explainers. We all struggle to find the best way to communicate our ideas and we sometimes fail. We can solve this problem, but first, we need to identify the root causes so we can build a foundation for solving them later.

All About Confidence

Those blank stares you see are a symptom of an underlying issue at the heart of why explanations fail. This issue is confidence, or the lack thereof. Blank stares often arise when someone has lost confidence that they can grasp—or should even care about—the idea you are communicating. And once confidence erodes, it is difficult to regain in that session. The audience essentially throws up their hands and focuses solely on "getting through" the explanation rather than fully understanding it. It can be a frustrating situation for all, and one that happens more than you think.

Assumptions Cause Failure

It can be easy to discern when an explanation is failing with a one-person audience. However, it can be more difficult to determine in a group meeting or classroom setting. For one thing, there are too many people present to gauge each one's engagement in your explanation. The real problem, however, is that you have no way of knowing each person's level of confidence in the material. For example, if your job is to explain type 2 diabetes to a large audience, it's nearly impossible to if they have never heard of the disorder before. What is basic to one person might be completely new information to another.

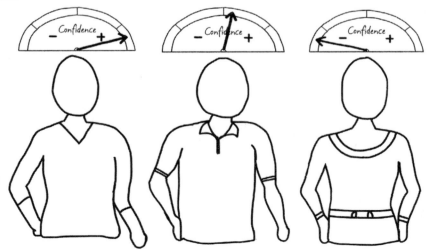

When you're faced with this, you must make assumptions about the confidence of the overall group, and inevitably, your assumptions will not match reality. This mismatch is common and probably the biggest reason explanations fail.

Of course, if we had a easy way to gauge every person's level of confidence in every subject, we might not need this book. For now, however, we have to make assumptions about the knowledge of people whom we may not know. And as we will see, we are generally not very skillful at doing so; therefore, we try to make up for it in other ways.

Why do we make such poor assumptions? To understand our problems in making assumptions, we can look at our decisions through the lens of the *curse of knowledge*, which is described in a book called *Made to Stick* by Chip and Dan Heath. The idea behind the curse of knowledge is that when we know a subject very well, we have a difficult time imagining what it is like *not* to know it. As we discussed previously, this is a matter of empathy. Our level of knowledge interferes with our ability to see the world from another person's perspective and gauge their confidence level accurately. We are cursed by what we already know. Here is an excerpt of an article by the authors from the *Harvard Business Review*:

In 1990, a Stanford University graduate student in psychology named Elizabeth Newton illustrated the curse of knowledge by studying a simple game in which she assigned people to one of two roles: "tapper" or "listener." Each tapper was asked to pick a well-known song, such as "Happy Birthday," and tap out the rhythm on a table. The listener's job was to guess the song.

Over the course of Newton's experiment, 120 songs were tapped out. Listeners guessed only three of the songs correctly: a success ratio of 2.5 percent. But before they guessed, Newton asked the tappers to predict the probability that listeners would guess correctly. They predicted 50 percent. The tappers got their message across one time in 40, but they thought they would get it across one time in two. Why?

When a tapper taps, it is impossible for her to avoid hearing the tune playing along to her taps. Meanwhile, all the listener can hear is a kind of bizarre Morse code. Yet the tappers were flabbergasted by how hard the listeners had to work to pick up the tune.

The problem is that once we know something—say, the melody of a song—we find it hard to imagine not knowing it. Our knowledge has "cursed" us. We have difficulty sharing it with others, because we can't readily re-create their state of mind.

In the business world, managers and employees, marketers and customers, corporate headquarters and the front line, all rely on ongoing communication but suffer from enormous information imbalances, just like the tappers and listeners.
        —Source: http://hbr.org/2006/12/the-curse-of-knowledge/ar/1

For example, this scenario is common when new employees enter a company. They may have stellar resumes and related experience, but this cannot prepare them for the organization's communication culture. In meeting after meeting, they encounter successful businesspeople who seem to speak another language while assuming they are being clear. Acronyms, product names, and processes flow from them without hesitation. They are assuming the tune is clear, but all the new employees hear is tap-tap-tap.

So when you are doing your best to explain an idea and see blank stares, it could be the curse of knowledge at work. You are tapping along to a tune you know well and assuming the other people can hear the same tune. But in reality, they're losing confidence—and your explanation is starting to fail.

As we will see in the following and throughout the book, the curse of knowledge is an underlying cause of numerous problems in explanations, something that cripples our ability to make accurate assumptions about our audience. Thankfully there are antidotes for the curse that can help us create explanations that account for it and build confidence.

Words Can Hurt

The curse of knowledge takes many forms. Consider, for example, the words you use every day in your job. Every profession, from medicine to woodworking, has its own language, and for good reason. We need this kind of specificity when we're at work; it gives us the ability to communicate with coworkers and peers without having to adjust for their confidence level. We can make accurate assumptions about the words they already understand because we work with them every day. Let's say that you work in the financial services field. You may use terms such as *amortization, depreciation,* and *vesting* so often you assume that everyone knows what they mean because pretty much everyone you work with *does.* The shared language becomes part of the workplace culture, and makes it more important and productive. However, it can also become a curse.

The more we live in a culture and use its own language, the more the curse of knowledge grows. Certain words and phrases become so common that we start to lose touch with how they sound to people who live outside of that culture. We may become prone to using a word like *transmogrify* or *quotidian* during a meeting or presentation and then wonder why there are blank stares when we use these same terms over dinner with our families.

A single word can make your explanation fail because it lowers confidence. One word has the power to move someone from interest to disinterest.

Think about it this way: you decide to get dinner at a new restaurant rumored to serve mouth-watering dishes. You open the menu and start to browse. If you are like most people, you're looking for dishes you either already like or would like to try. The menu's job is to be your guide, to serve as a resource that helps you make a decision with confidence. You narrow the choices to three dishes, and ponder the elements of each:

1. Sea bass with wild rice and greens
2. Ribeye steak with garlic mashed potatoes and grilled asparagus
3. Crab cakes with mushrooms and a French rémoulade

Although they all sound delicious, the third option feels like a risk. You have never seen the word *rémoulade* before, so you are not sure if you would like it. Therefore, you decide against ordering the entire dish because this one word made your confidence wane. You know that you love crab cakes and mushrooms, but the third part—rémoulade—moved you from interest to disinterest. It is an unknown element that represented a reason, in your mind, to move it to the bottom of the list.

This might seem like a tragedy to the rémoulade lovers out there, but it serves as an example for explanations: the words we use *matter*. In reality, rémoulade is a lot like tartar sauce, but sounds much more appealing and sophisticated on a menu. However, for the uninformed, it represents a reason to disregard an entire dish.

Explanations fail when we are unable to translate the language of our work to the language of a possibly uninformed audience. The curse of knowledge changes our perceptions and makes it difficult to make accurate assumptions about what others may know.

We Lack Understanding

The curse of knowledge can be a privilege for some because it assumes that a person knows *too much*. But what about the other side of the coin? Knowing too little is an obvious problem when it comes to explanation. As Einstein once said, "If you can't explain it simply, you don't understand it well enough." (BrainyQuote, 2012.) Being in the explanation business, I've learned that approaching an explanation without sufficient understanding is a quick way to dig yourself into a hole. The key to avoiding this situation is to set expectations.

For example, say you saw a news story about a new cancer drug that's coming onto the market. You're no scientist, but from the news story you get a pretty good understanding of the basics of the new drug. Because you're excited, you want to share the information. There is no harm in sharing—we all do it at times without fully understanding an idea. The problem arises when you position yourself as a knowledgeable person or use the word *explain*, as in, "I can explain it to you." This gives your audience a signal that you have the information they need. Without realizing it, you've become an authority, which comes with a responsibility to make things clear and accurate. However, the news story gave you some surface-level information, but didn't provide enough to truly understand the drug. Of course, this will become abundantly clear once you've shared the facts you know and are asked for more information. At this point you're forced to admit you don't know the answers, or, even worse, you make things up to appear smart.

The key here is realizing that explanation means something to an audience and the word should be used with care. If you understand a subject and are prepared to answer questions, you are set up for success. But if you lack the understanding needed to converse about the subject and frame your ideas as an explanation, your lack of knowledge can easily be discovered and cause your explanation to fail.

We Want to Appear Smart

There are experts in almost any profession—people who are known as leaders in a specific field. They write groundbreaking scientific papers, their art is respected by critics, and their companies flourish. We admire them and feel inspired by them. Although we may not know them personally, they are in the backs of our minds, constantly looking over our shoulders. We imagine what they would think of our work and would love a chance to earn their approval.

These individuals' impressive achievements motivate a number of professionals, which is a productive part of life. However, the need to appeal to experts also has the potential to make our explanations fail.

Dipika is a rising star at her organization. With a freshly minted MBA in her possession, she is brimming with ideas about marketing and has been working on a presentation for other teams in the company that will help them understand a possible marketing strategy for the next few years.

Dipika realized while preparing for her presentation that the Chief Marketing Officer would be attending, which made her heart skip a beat. The CMO is known as one of the global experts in corporate marketing, and to have her at the meeting is an honor and is also terrifying. The stakes were high, and Dipika knew she had to make a good impression.

She felt confident on the day of the meeting. Public speaking had always come naturally to her, and her education granted her a solid technical foundation in marketing. She imagined engineers and designers suddenly understanding marketing from a new perspective once she'd given her presentation. Executives would surely be blown away by her depth of knowledge, and the CMO would certainly be ready to promote her to the executive suite on the spot!

With all eyes on her, she stepped up to the projector light and dove into the presentation. A wave of confidence washed over Dipika as she illustrated each of her ideas with charts and graphs and narrated her presentation using the language of marketing. She saved a few minutes after her presentation and opened the floor for questions, at which point she was met with silence and blank stares. She nervously told the audience members that she was happy to look at anything more closely, even after the meeting.

Dipika met with her boss the following day to debrief the presentation. He said her presentation was accurate, beautifully designed, and filled with great information. Then he said carefully, "However, many of your insightful ideas were incomprehensible to most of the people in the room."

Dipika's heart fell. What had gone wrong? How could she have missed the mark by so much?

To help diagnose the problem, her boss asked her who she was thinking about when she was creating the presentation. Dipika knew the right answer: the various teams at the company. Unfortunately, she also knew the real answer—and so did

(continued)

(continued)

her boss. A quick discussion allowed her to see that her perspective had changed the moment she learned that the CMO was planning to attend. She started to see the presentation as a perfect chance to impress someone she respected and admired, rather than an opportunity to clarify concepts for her colleagues.

Dipika's boss assured her that although the CMO *was* impressed with the content, it was clear that her presentation was not focused on the rest of the audience's needs. Dipika had traded the opportunity to build confidence among the teams for one to impress the experts.

As Dipika learned, this is a poor trade-off in most situations. At heart, her presentation had potential; however, it was ineffective because its goal was to make her *look* smart, instead of helping others *feel* smart. This became the real lesson, and in the future, Dipika concentrated on impressing experts by her ability to help everyone in the room feel smarter.

The Direct Approach—No Context

Most people take explanation for granted. Because it's something we do every day in one form or another, we rarely take a step back and think about how we present an idea. When someone asks us, "How does that work?" or "Why does that happen?" we tend to answer the question directly if we know the answer. After all, it is efficient. Another person asks a question; we provide the answer to their question. It is usually a win-win.

The problem with this is that the direct approach can have an unintended consequence: the loss of confidence. Although their question wanted for an *explanation,* what they received was a statement of fact. Why does oil float on top of water in a glass? Relative density. What causes climate change? Increased CO_2 in the atmosphere. Why does the ocean have tides? The moon.

Giving direct, accurate, and factual answers may seem to solve the problem from the perspective of the answerer. But in reality, it can shut the asker down. A statement of fact with no other context puts the onus on the asker to take the next step. If the asker isn't familiar with relative density or CO_2, they are likely to move on rather than ask a follow-up question or probe for related ideas. Any hope of becoming a customer of that idea is lost.

This is a failure in the form of a lost opportunity. Although direct answers are often needed and well-placed, they do not work universally. A skilled explainer learns to see the intent behind the question and formulate an answer that focuses on understanding instead of efficiency. They answer questions like "What is this?" as if the question was, "Why should I care about this?" You can see this in play in the following example.

In 2004, I attended a small conference in Silicon Valley that brought together technologists, executives, and consultants. The second day of the conference began with the CEO of a technology company speaking about some trends that he saw on the Web. Along with blogs and wikis, he mentioned RSS a few times.

An older gentleman who had an engineering background raised his hand after the CEO mentioned RSS for the third time and posed the seemingly simple question: "What is RSS?"

The CEO looked at him and blithely offered the following definition: "Oh, RSS is an XML-based content syndication format." With a quick nod, the engineer's hand went down and the CEO moved on to the next subject.

Despite being 100 percent accurate, the CEO's explanation failed the engineer and most of the people in the room. It was too direct and didn't provide any information that the engineer could use to make sense of RSS.

Sadly, the CEO probably did not have any idea what happened. From his perspective, he provided the most accurate and succinct answer possible. His priority was efficiency and he likely assumed it was effective. But it was not helpful at all from the engineer's perspective. In fact, it made him feel *less* confident that RSS was something he was capable of understanding.

Again, this is a lost opportunity. The CEO did not recognize that the engineer needed an explanation or that the direct answer he gave could actually cause more problems. He assumed that the direct approach would be the best way to answer and let him get back to his presentation. Had he heard "What is RSS" and answered a slightly different question, such as "Why should I care about RSS?" he could have helped the engineer feel confident. In this scenario, he could have replied "RSS makes it easy to subscribe to websites so that new content comes directly to you."

This scenario unfolds every day in almost every company. We all answer questions; our challenge is to answer in the form that will help the person who's asking the most. Unfortunately, thanks to the curse of knowledge, we assume too often that the audience will be able to make sense of direct answers, when in reality, they usually need an explanation.

Summary

At heart, explanations are about affecting confidence. Good ones build it, and poor ones diminish or even eliminate it—and there is no shortage of ways to lose confidence. So what do we do? How do we address these problems and learn to build confidence through our explanations? The answer is simple: we start planning.

CHAPTER 4

Planning Your Explanations

A few years ago, my wife Sachi and I renovated our house. We saw an opportunity to transform it into a home *and* office. One of the first steps in this process was to spend time with an architect who gave us a sense of what was possible. This focus on planning meant that we could:

- Create and analyze the house's look and function
- Anticipate and account for potential problems
- Visually understand the big picture

This planning process helped the completed house become much more tangible to us. What was formerly a set of ideas with direction now had a form. We could begin the process of diving a little deeper into the details. Once we knew where the walls, windows, and doorways would be, we could think about lighting and electrical.

The need to have plans in construction is obvious: they save time and money. But what about in communication? How often do we sit down and focus on how we will explain an idea? What if planning our explanations could give form to our communications and yield better results, similar to those we enjoy when planning a home renovation?

This chapter will discuss the role of planning in building better explanations, and will introduce a model that will become one of our most valuable tools. We'll start by taking a look at the process of identifying problems because that is what plans do—help solve them.

Identifying Explanation Problems

Sachi and I came up with the idea of renovating our house after living there and seeing where design and function could be better. For example, the house's design of narrow hallways and small intimate rooms inhibited our ability to work together in the same room. We knew we could address that problem—and several others—through renovation.

Our lives as professionals are filled with potential problems as well. Some may be political: we can't move forward on a project without a boss's approval. Some may be financial: the company can't afford to do everything. Some may be technical: we don't have the tools or know-how to complete a particular project. Perhaps the biggest problem is time: there are not enough hours in the day.

Although most of us recognize the solutions for these common situations, there is another kind of problem that is perhaps more pervasive than any of those listed previously. It is so common that we do not realize it is there. It is the explanation problem.

An explanation problem is related to how we choose to communicate ideas. What makes an explanation problem so insidious is that it has the power to ruin the best, most productive, life changing ideas in just a few sentences.

A great idea, poorly explained, ceases to appear great, and the cost is tremendous. Let us consider the cost to the technology industry in the following example.

Meet Andre. He graduated from Stanford University a few years ago with a degree in computer science and is now focused on the company he started that he hopes will change the world. He and a handful of employees have been working on a product for more than a year now, and it is finally coming to life. Technically, it's an amazing product with the potential to positively impact millions of people—and Andre is finally ready to share it with the world.

Andre knows every detail of his product. He's prepared to answer any question and to speak about it with passion. After all, he's been able to overcome every challenge so far. His team of engineers solved the technical problems, his designers made it easy to use, and his investors, including a couple of angel investors, helped him overcome the financial limitations. If he can get a good start by word of mouth, the product is likely to spread virally from one person to another.

Andre's company finally arrived at launch day and the team was psyched. They were about to publish the website and announce the product to the world. All their work had come to this moment, and it seemed to go off perfectly. The first 48 hours were amazing. People were signing up rapidly and there was significant buzz online. It looked like things were going well.

But after the first month, new sign-ups leveled off and started to drop. Andre and the team were concerned; they started to analyze the data to determine why this was happening. The website hadn't changed, and the features were the same. What could it be?

The team decided to talk to some of the product's early users to see if they could offer additional insight. These users were a part of the product's tech-savvy market segment, and they were obviously excited about it. In fact, it seemed their excitement was contagious—just what Andre wanted. However, one thing became clear when interviewing these users: although they understood the product and its value well, they couldn't explain it in a way that encouraged others who were less tech-savvy to be interested. The excitement about the product's features was not translating to the people who could benefit from it. It was obvious that users weren't adopting the product because it was difficult to explain. Andre and the team could see that they had an explanation problem.

(continued)

(*continued*)

They had spent so much time and money developing the product and solving the financial and technical problems that they hadn't considered how to package the big idea of the product in a way that would help it spread from person-to-person. They assumed that it would be self-explanatory, with early users communicating its value to the rest of the market. However, the deeper they dug, the more they saw that the decline in sign-ups was because the product had only reached the initial adopters. Once that core group of users signed up, adoption stopped.

In some ways, this was a relief for Andre and the team because it provided them with evidence that the product was well-designed and the features worked. They didn't need to rethink the product; however, they *did* need to craft their communication strategy. How could their product make it from the inner circle of early adopters out to the mainstream?

At first it seemed like a marketing problem. Perhaps they needed to rebrand the product or change the copy on the website. They wondered if the tagline or the logo wasn't working. However, after considering those elements, it still didn't feel right. After all, early adopters were not going to change their communication style based on marketing terminology. The team needed to provide an explanation that accounted for everyone—not just the early adopters. In fact, it needed to be one that early adopters could *use* to help get others interested.

No one on the team had ever considered solving this important problem. How do you create an explanation that makes people care? They needed a plan.

Andre's situation is not unique to technology or to startup businesses. We all have ideas, products, and services that are often of high quality on their own merit. The problem we face is not one of features, design, or intellect, but one of explanation: how we relate the ideas to others. Without a way to explain something effectively, we limit its ability to spread.

Fortunately, we can all use the following simple model, called the "explanation scale," to develop a plan for solving explanation problems. This model provides a way to visualize the audience, account for their needs, and move them from misunderstanding to understanding via a carefully crafted explanation. So let's take a look.

The simple A-to-Z continuum will be our guide to planning explanations. It is a simple way to think about moving your audience from one point to another. We will use this scale throughout the rest of the book to think about the transition from less understanding to more understanding of a concept. Therefore, it is important that we start with the big, basic ideas.

A B C D E F G H I J K L M N O P Q R S T U V W X Y Z

LESS UNDERSTANDING   MORE UNDERSTANDING

For example, the figure in the following is currently at "C" on the less understanding end of the scale. The arrow shows that our goal is to move her from left to right on the scale, representing her path to understanding an idea.

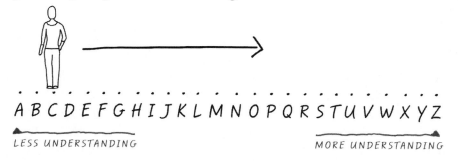

A B C D E F G H I J K L M N O P Q R S T U V W X Y Z

LESS UNDERSTANDING   MORE UNDERSTANDING

This scale is a part of the core of this book and is the instrument we use to map an explanation. We'll plot most of the ideas we discuss from this point forward on it, thereby creating a simple, memorable and visual tool for thinking about and planning explanations.

Back to Andre's explanation problem.

Andre's team has now identified that they have an explanation problem: their product's adoption is being limited by how it is being explained.

Therefore, the team decides to start with themselves. As the developers, they understand the product completely, so they plot themselves at the far right of the

(continued)

(continued)

scale, around the "Y" mark. They've learned from talking to the early adopters that they also understand the product very well, and are far down on the scale as well—around the "U" mark. The scale looks like this:

It is clear that those who will be doing the explaining are very informed. They understand the product and feel confident about their knowledge. Of course, as discussed in Chapter 3, experience is not always an asset when it comes to explanation. It is likely that both Andre's team and the early adopters are suffering from the curse of knowledge: they know the product so well that it is difficult for them to imagine what it must be like *not* to understand it. The curse gets stronger the further you move towards "Z" on the scale, which can cause multiple problems.

First, the team is more likely to make incorrect assumptions about what people already understand. Second, early adopters are more likely to use technical language to describe features and benefits without adjusting for those with less experience. These factors may be the source of the adoption problem Andre is experiencing: the explainers are not accounting for those at the other end of the scale.

It starts to become clear for Andre: the people who understand and believe in the product are all the way at the right end of the scale—and everyone there has the curse of knowledge. At the same time, the market for the product is very broad; Andre sees that most of his potential users are all over the scale, from "A" to at least "N."

Andre is able to use the scale to see the wide gulf between the people who understand the product and those who do not. He has to make assumptions about his target market. Because the product is meant to be mainstream, he must assume that the people in his target market fall everywhere on the scale of understanding.

Andre must then consider the assumptions he and the early adopters have been making about people's existing knowledge of the product. Through discussions and interviews with current users, his team is able to get a feel for how the product is currently being explained. They use this information to decide that the current explanations assume that people have at least an understanding of level "L."

From here, it is obvious what is happening. Thanks to the curse of knowledge, Andre's team and the early adopters are making assumptions—incorrect ones—about what people already understand. Their explanations appeal to the most informed of the target market, but leave the majority of potential users behind. As the following scale illustrates, the mainstream is not being reached by the current explanations.

(continued)

(continued)

Once he sees his market mapped along this scale, Andre understands that explanations were limiting his product's potential. He and his team had been working on it for so long they lost touch with the market and could not explain the product in a way that made potential customers feel confident that they could use it.

Now that Andre is aware of the explanation problem, his mind turns immediately to solutions—and some big questions come to mind:

- How do you know where to *start* an explanation?
- How do you account for people at every point on the scale?
- What ideas and tactics make explanations work?
- How do you get people down the scale?

In this context, I invite you to think about your own situation. Although Andre happens to be an entrepreneur, this scale serves as a way to think about almost any explanation problem that people encounter. Ask yourself the following:

- Where are you on the scale regarding a specific idea?
- Where is your audience?
- What assumptions are you making about their level of understanding?
- Are your current explanations accounting for everyone on the scale?
- Should they?

These questions are important because they frame perhaps the biggest problem in communication: we make poor assumptions about what people already know, and these assumptions limit the potential of our explanations. By using the explanation scale, we have a simple way to think about, talk through, and plan our explanations.

Next we'll look at how we can package our ideas into explanations that help us answer the previous questions and see how to think about building confidence via stepping stones that move the audience down the scale with confidence.

**EXPLANATIONS AT WORK: ALBERT NI AND 25 MILLION VIEWS
ON DROPBOX.COM**

In 2009, we were connected with a startup called Dropbox, which was looking for a video that would explain their product. The company was growing at an incredible rate and saw the potential for a short explanation to encourage more people to try the product. After using Dropbox and talking with the founders, we came to a couple of conclusions:

1. Dropbox is an amazingly simple tool that solves a real problem
2. It's very hard to explain. You don't realize you need it until you use it.

For us, this was a great challenge. We agreed to work with founders Drew Houston and Arash Ferdowsi on the video, not knowing how it would be used. In the fall of 2009, the Dropbox homepage was redesigned and featured our video as the main content. At the time of writing, 2.5 years later, the company has over 200 million users and the video is still on the Dropbox home page. According to Albert Ni, the former analytics lead at Dropbox, the video has been viewed about 25 million times. That's a lot of explaining!

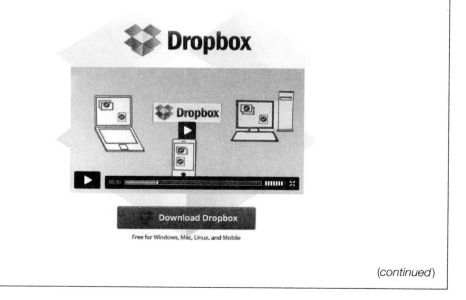

(*continued*)

(continued)

Recently I spoke with Ni (who now manages multiple teams) about the video and what role it plays on the front page:

For us the rationale has been simple — we wanted to give people a chance to understand what Dropbox was. A lot of people had already heard of Dropbox when they hit www.dropbox.com, but a lot of other people might have stumbled upon it. We've seen evidence over and over again that Dropbox often fits into the category of things that "you don't know you need," because for the less tech-savvy, it's totally unclear that something like Dropbox could even exist and they don't even know to want it. We feel the video does a good job bridging that gap. The fact that it can take someone from having no idea whatsoever what Dropbox is to having a sense of how it could be useful to them makes it very valuable for a significant subset of our visitors.

This is explanation at work. The Dropbox team realized that people coming to their website needed a way to understand Dropbox and get a "sense of how it could be useful." I'm biased, but I think almost every technology website needs a video explanation doing this.

PART 2

Package

CHAPTER 5

Packaging Ideas

You have learned so far that explanation problems prevent people from understanding one another's ideas. Using the explanation scale, you learned to picture people who lack understanding on the "A" end of the scale. You know you need ways to move them closer to the "Z" end with confidence.

The second part of this book is dedicated to packaging ideas into explanations that can help you move people across the scale with ease. Many of these tactics were identified through making Common Craft videos, which we see as 3-minute packages of ideas. In creating more than 100 video explanations for companies and educators, we have analyzed and refined the main factors that make ideas easy to understand.

The idea of packaging works because packages have limits. Only so many things can fit into a package, and this is true with explanations as well. By packaging ideas into explanations, we define the package's contents by what we include or exclude.

This gives our explanation form, shape, and limits. The idea is to identify an explanation problem and build a package that will solve it through explanation.

Below is the explanation scale that Andre's team used to visualize the reach of their current explanations. It highlighted a large group of potential customers on the "A" end of the scale who were left out because the curse of knowledge prevented Andre's team from accounting for their needs.

Stepping Outside the Bubble

Andre and his team have realized they need to package ideas into easy-to-understand explanations that start on the "A" end of the scale. But he has some concerns. He is a smart guy who works with smart people. As such, he prefers expressing his ideas in the industry's vernacular when he speaks, demonstrating his knowledge and intelligence. He believes it is an important skill for the leader of a company to exhibit.

When he thinks about explaining his product for someone at the "A" end of the scale, he worries that his message will be "dumbed down." Andre has received little reward in simplifying his language and ideas for most of his life; in contrast, his professors and bosses encouraged him to flex his intellectual muscles. This context taught him to see dumbing down as a weakness—one that wasted time and could offend the experts whose respect you need.

This phenomenon is very common in both academia and business. You only need to read an academic paper or listen to the acronyms used in a business meeting to experience it. It does have value: industry experts need to communicate in their own language to relate specific and detailed information. For example, the medical terms used in an emergency department must be direct and specific to be effective. The same is true on an oil rig or in the kitchen of a restaurant. What often appears as complex communication is just deeply specific and meant for a narrow audience. And this kind of communication is understandable inside the bubble of expertise.

Andre notices his team developing an intimate language inside a bubble of their own as they're building the product. Their words, shortcuts, and acronyms have become common throughout their offices and cubicles. This intimacy of language has played a valuable role in interacting with each other efficiently. Because every team member is at "X," "Y," or "Z" on the explanation scale, there is no need to repeat the big ideas; everyone already understands them. This would be redundant and wasteful inside the bubble. But now that the product is almost ready for its mainstream audience, this communication style becomes a liability instead of an asset.

Andre imagines his team inside the product bubble, talking in the language they've developed. He then imagines his future users outside the bubble—people at the "A" end of the scale. This image helps him see that a big part of his success will depend on transforming ideas, concepts, and features from inside the bubble into a form that will make sense to these outside users. The membrane of the bubble is an important barrier for Andre and the team because they're likely to confuse people if they cross it without thinking. But if they can prepare for crossing it, they'll be able to step out into the real world using communications that help potential users feel confident and smart.

(continued)

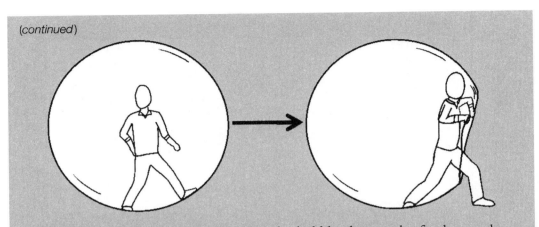

(continued)

Andre realized for the first time that the bubble changes the fundamental way he and his team think about communication. Inside it, the team needs specificity, acronyms, and details; people are rewarded for using their communication to flex their intellectual muscles. This inward orientation rewards looking smart.

But everything changes outside the bubble. They have to rein in the need to look smart and they must think differently. To succeed here, they must focus on helping others *feel* smart. This idea was a revelation, especially to Andre.

The question becomes: how will they do this? Andre's team comprises mostly programmers and developers. They all see the potential, but aren't sure where to start when it comes to making their ideas easier and clearer for other people.

The answer for Andre's team—and for all people who want to make their ideas easier for others to understand—is packaging. They need to consider the potential to take a big idea or set of ideas and exhibit them in a form that solves an explanation problem for people outside the bubble.

What Goes into the Packaging?

Packaging ideas is a simple process that requires the person presenting ideas to account for the audience's needs. And because every audience and idea is different, there are innumerable ways to package ideas. However, they all focus on a few important elements:

Agreement—Agreement builds confidence from the very first sentence. It is accomplished through big-picture statements that most people will recognize. These are ideas about which you can say something like, "We can all agree that gas prices are rising."

Context—Context moves the points we have agreed upon into a specific place. It gives the audience a foundation for the explanation and lets them know why it should matter to them. For instance, you could say, "More of your hard earned income is going to pay for transportation."

Story—Story applies the big ideas to a narrative that shows a person who experiences a change in perspective and the emotions that accompany that change. "Meet Sally; she's tired of paying so much for gas and needs alternatives. Here's what she found."

Connections—Connections often accompany a story and are analogies and metaphors that connect new ideas to something people already understand. "Sally could see that taking the bus was like multitasking because she could work and commute at the same time."

Descriptions—Descriptions are direct communications that are more focused on how versus why. "Sally found that she could save more than $20 a week by taking the bus three times weekly."

Conclusion—Conclusion wraps up the package with a summary of what was learned and provides a next step with a focus on the audience. "The next time gas prices get you down, remember . . ."

The examples above are high-level guidelines we'll explore more fully in following chapters. For now, it's important to think about these elements as stepping-stones in an explanation, with each step moving the audience from "A" to "Z" with confidence.

A B C D E F G H I J K L M N O P Q R S T U V W X Y Z

LESS UNDERSTANDING   MORE UNDERSTANDING

CHAPTER 6

Context

Like explanation itself, context is a part of our everyday language. It is an important part of making an idea, fact, or story more understandable and useful. Like the illustration at the beginning of the chapter, I see context as a foundational element of communication—it provides a place for people and ideas to come together. Applied properly, context allows ideas to come alive and to be applied in new ways. Unfortunately, context is often forgotten or limited. This makes our ideas appear to be inside jokes, in which the punchline requires previous knowledge.

For example, imagine you are meeting friends for a beer. You arrive to find them deep in conversation. Not wanting to interrupt, you sit down quietly and listen in.

Over a few minutes, you gather some information. They're talking about sports, and you hear names such as Chelsea and Arsenal, leading you to believe they are talking about English Premier League Soccer. Then you hear more names such as Barcelona and Juventus. Slowly, a picture emerges in your mind based on a set of clues, but you're not sure how to proceed. The problem is that you have no *context*. The clues you see have no foundation—they are adrift in your mind, which is working hard to make sense of it all.

Then your friend turns to you and says "Oh, sorry, we're talking about UEFA Champions League, which brings together the best teams of Europe. Specifically, we're talking about the English teams and how they are doing in league play."

Suddenly it all becomes clear. Two sentences from your friend gave the whole discussion a foundation built on context. With this foundation, the clues you heard became connected and were no longer adrift in your mind. Now you can listen with greater interest and even contribute without worry.

This simple example highlights another important idea in this book: context matters. Our ideas may be useful, actionable, and informative, but without context, they are limited. If they exist without a foundation or connection to other ideas, they are isolated, and that isolation limits their potential.

You have probably heard the saying, "You're missing the forest for the trees." It means you are so focused on the details that you are missing the big picture. This applies directly to the idea of context in explanation. Trees are great and can be very helpful, but information about the forest makes them useful.

In the previous story, the team names are trees, which are helpful clues. But a few words about the forest (English performance in the UEFA Champions League) makes them useful.

The problem is we neglect to include enough context when relating ideas. Inside the bubble, everything is a tree and context isn't needed—everyone knows the forest. But when we step out of the bubble, everything changes, and we have to focus on the forest to make our ideas understandable. As my friend Tony O'Driscoll reminded me recently, content is king, but context is the *kingdom*.

Let's look at a story that puts the big ideas into action.

Forest then Trees

Angela had been working in a number of part-time jobs since graduating from school, and she was ready for something new. She spent some time as a cashier, a barista, and even a florist, where she picked up some valuable skills. But she wants a new, career-oriented challenge these days. After talking to some friends and family, she identified accounting as a possible path for her future. She loves working with numbers and has great attention to detail, both good skills for accountants. But there was a problem: she didn't have any experience as an accountant. Although she's worked for most of her life, she's never been involved in managing a business's finances.

She saw some ads in her local newspaper for accounting workshops, which sounded like a good first step. When the first day of the workshop arrived, she walked in with a positive outlook.

The instructor hurried in and spread his coat and bag on the front desk. Angela thought he actually looked like an accountant, even though she couldn't quite explain why. His name was Mr. Tidwell and he introduced himself as a long-time accountant and teacher of accounting. Angela took a deep breath and opened her book as instructed.

Within an hour, however, Angela could feel her confidence start to wane. Although an able accountant and teacher, Mr. Tidwell was describing tools and terms that didn't sound familiar to her: credits, debits, revenues, and expenses. At first it seemed manageable; after all, she could memorize their definitions and certainly pick them out of a multiple choice test. However, she felt like something was missing. She wasn't sure how to apply them in any practical way. What made matters worse was that her classmates seemed to understand without any trouble. They nodded and took notes as Mr. Tidwell lectured.

As time went on, relying on memorization become more of a liability. Was depreciation a debit or credit? The faster information was relayed, the harder it became to keep up. Once the class reached the topic of financial statements, she

(continued)

(*continued*)

started to panic. How did anyone know how this fit together? Is it the accountant's job to know how all this works? All Angela knew was that she felt frustrated and discouraged. Maybe she wasn't smart enough to be an accountant after all.

One night over appetizers and cocktails, she described her experience to a friend who listened to her story and empathized. Because Angela's friend had taken accounting in college, she knew that it was a subject that you must "get" for it to make sense, and she could tell that Angela wasn't getting it. She encouraged Angela to try again with a different workshop and teacher. Feeling a bit more confident, Angela decided to give it a try.

A few weeks later she entered the now-familiar classroom, hoping for better results. To her amazement, this instructor looked as if she could be Mr. Tidwell's sister. But Ms. Stowe was no Mr. Tidwell.

After a quick introduction of her impressive credentials, she started the class from a completely different perspective: by asking the class to talk about their experiences in business. A few people described their previous jobs, and Ms. Stowe used these examples to talk about how businesses run. In the first few hours, Angela didn't hear the word *debit* once. Instead, she learned about the basics of business. Ms. Stowe talked about what is needed for businesses to survive. She talked about how money flows through the company, what must happen to make a profit, and how profit makes businesses successful. Although Angela had been around businesses her whole life, she had never thought about the big picture in this way.

The first day of this workshop couldn't have been more different from Mr. Tidwell's class. Angela went home excited and confident. She hadn't yet learned anything specific about accounting, but she did have a basic understanding of how businesses manage money and why management is necessary.

Ms. Stowe introduced the same subjects that Mr. Tidwell had over the next few workshops, but in a slightly different way. She presented ideas such as debits and credits in the context of managing a business. The light bulb was starting to shine for Angela, and it wasn't just about memorization this time. She could picture the money flowing through the business and how accounting worked to make it manageable. "Of course office supplies are an expense," she thought. "*Now* it makes sense."

Within a few weeks Angela completed the workshop with flying colors. She wasn't quite ready to be a CPA, but she had the tools and the confidence to take the next step.

Angela's story likely sounds familiar. You may have walked into a classroom or presentation and felt blindsided by a presenter who focused only on ideas without using a context that connected the ideas to a foundation. For Angela, the ideas were debits and credits; for others, this might be hearing about a product's features without hearing why it would be useful or receiving business data without understanding the company's strategy.

Mr. Tidwell's approach to explaining accounting failed Angela because he focused only on the trees. Debits and credits are important, but he never connected them to the forest. Ms. Stowe, on the other hand, started with the forest. She spent time on the big picture: the world in which accounting operates. This gave Angela context for understanding the trees of debits and credits and why they make sense in this world.

One way to think about Angela's story is on the explanation scale. Because she was starting at the "A" end, she needed the forest. But as she progressed, she was more prepared for the trees:

A B C D E F G H I J K L M N O P Q R S T U V W X Y Z

LESS UNDERSTANDING   MORE UNDERSTANDING

Another way to think about context and the explanation scale is by understanding that explanations often cover questions of both *how* and *why*. In Angela's example, she needed to see *why* first, but as she moved down the scale, *how* became more important. We can plot this progression on the scale and see how the balance of *why* and *how* changes at any point:

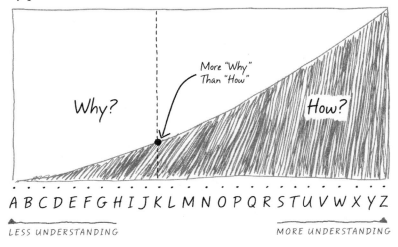

Solving the Context Problem

The ability to use context effectively in an explanation is based on knowing your audience or accounting for an audience with mixed levels of knowledge. For example, teachers may have a good idea of what their students know and don't know. If you've been invited to present at a conference, however, you may know very little about the audience for your explanation. The organizers likely didn't give you more than a cursory overview of the attendees and their interests. It's up to you to get it right in your attempts to answer the following questions:

How do you find the right amount of context?
How do you estimate the audience's existing knowledge?
How do you impress both the experts *and* the beginners?

Let's cover these questions by using a story.

BEGINNERS THEN EXPERTS: Paolo and the Conference Presentation

Paolo is a bright guy. A few years back, he graduated from a top university with a degree in computer science. He's been conducting research in the field of genetics since then, which is increasingly focused on the use of powerful computers. Paolo's friends know him as a friendly, sincere guy, but one with an intellect that sometimes gets in the way of conversations. He frequently talks over their heads and doesn't even realize it.

For the past year, Paolo has been working on a project that could become big news in his field. After publishing some initial findings, he was invited to present his work at a variety of conferences. Although he's an able presenter, like almost everyone he has some stage fright. He's 100 percent confident in his work and the project, but he knows he has a difficult time explaining what he does. The conferences usually attract audiences with a wide range of expertise and often include well-known experts in his field. As a young expert, he's motivated to present himself and explain his project in the most flattering way possible.

Paolo remembers while preparing for his first talk that the university is well-known for innovative genetics research. He uses this information to craft a presentation in the language of genetics researchers. From the opening slide, he dives into a common genetics dilemma, assuming the audience possesses a level of knowledge similar to his. Referring to influential papers and important discoveries and using acronyms, he fills the allotted time with as much information as he can. He smiles with pride, sure that the audience will be impressed by the depth of his knowledge.

Paolo feels good throughout the presentation. The information flows smoothly and the audience seems to be paying attention. He allows for a few minutes at the end and opens the floor for questions.

A younger man rises for the first question and asks something completely unexpected: a question about the role of computers in genetics. This floors Paolo. His entire presentation was about that very subject! How could a person at this prestigious university have missed the central message of his talk? He answers the question and feels a bit shaken.

(continued)

(continued)

Following the formalities of the session, he mingles with the other presenters, many of whom are his peers. Those Paolo speaks to, including a few real luminaries in his field, are very impressed by his work. They now understand the intimate details of his research and feel inspired by it. This adds a spring in his step. His presentation impressed those whom he respected.

Paolo and a group of friends head out on the town that night. The group includes a mix of people, some who are in his field, others who are not. He asks each of his friends to give their honest perspectives on his session. At first they all say it was interesting and well-presented; however, the more he presses them, the more he realizes they didn't comprehend the big ideas. From his observation, only one or two people at the table took valuable information from his presentation. He starts feeling a mix of emotions. Was his presentation too one-sided? Was it incomprehensible to the majority of people in the audience? Had he confused the masses to please the few?

If Paolo plans to build a career on this work, he needs and wants for it to inspire people. But how? How can he explain his work so that an audience of both experts and beginners can get excited about it?

Paolo asks around and meets a communications consultant who helps him think about his presentations a little differently. They discuss his preparation and how he perceives the audience. It becomes clear that he was focusing on impressing the experts in the room. He's built his life around becoming an expert in his field, and he sees these presentations as a chance to demonstrate that he has become one. Because he spends so much time researching, he assumes that the audience has a similar level of expertise—that they live in the same bubble that he does. He believes it would be detrimental to his career to speak in terms that are too basic. Therefore, he amps up the expertise via added details.

It becomes clear when he analyzes his presentation with the consultant. It's likely that the majority of the people in the room were lost. The young man who raised his hand probably represented the majority who didn't understand enough to ask an appropriate question.

It also becomes clear to Paolo that something has to change. He needs a new path and a couple of thought exercises help him gain a new perspective on his presentations.

The consultant asks Paolo to think about the audience as ten people in a room: two people with little interest, six people with interest but little expertise, and two experts.

His challenge is to reach these people with a one-hour presentation. Paolo assumes that it will be difficult to do so without making a poor impression on the experts who matter most to him; however, by following the exercise, he can see how this may not be the case.

The consultant instructs Paolo to think about the presentation in terms of cost, such as the cost of a negative impression. Each time his presentation doesn't meet his audience members' needs, it will cost him. Of course, the challenge is finding the right balance because everything he says could potentially cost something. If it's too complex for one person, the cost would be small, but multiplied across eight people, the cost adds up. If it's too simplistic, one expert may cost him a lot. So what can he do?

When he looks back at his presentation, Paolo can see that he decided to impress the experts. And he paid for it—the majority walked away confused, and he surely made a negative impression on the beginners. This approach had a high cost.

(continued)

(continued)

But he has an epiphany. When he was a student, his classes sometimes overlapped. As a result, he learned the same ideas more than once; but it didn't bother him. Different professors had different perspectives on the same ideas, and in most cases, the repetition of those ideas he already understood simply *validated* his own. Reviewing the basics is part of the academic process.

He reconsiders the expert side in terms of costs. There isn't anything *negative* about rehashing the basics. Will the experts mind or think poorly of him for taking the time to explain the big ideas that build the foundation of his work? Probably not. As the consultant explains, the cost of building context is *low* because it doesn't create a negative experience for anyone; it simply validates their knowledge or helps them feel confident. The cost of context is low and the benefits are high.

For the first time, Paolo sees how he overestimated the cost of covering the basics and helping the beginners get up to speed. He considers his next presentation and declares his first priority is to help get everyone in the room on the same page.

Standing in front of his second audience, he starts at the beginning. He asks the audience to raise their hand if they recognize the terms on the screen. Some hands go up, but they're scattered throughout the room and fewer than he expected. This allows him to adjust his starting point for a novice level of expertise. He then launches his presentation from a high level and focuses on where his work fits into the world, what he hopes to accomplish, and who it could impact. He speaks more plainly and gives examples with which he hopes all audience members can identify.

After taking the time to introduce his work, he dives a little deeper, and then a little deeper still. He doesn't expect everyone to follow every thought, but at least he gives everyone in the room a reason to be interested and learn more. He feels much better about the session and answers multiple questions afterward that demonstrate his audience understood the big ideas.

This time, his peers congratulate him on a successful presentation. But more importantly, they commend him on his ability to help everyone in the room see the importance of his work and how they could be involved. For him, this was a bigger win than he could have expected.

Context matters in this example—the *right* context. Paolo was able to see that his time was well-spent building context because it brought the majority of the group up to speed without compromising his standing among peers.

Context in Explanation—We Can All Agree

Using context effectively is one of the most powerful skills for an explainer because it is an invitation to stay engaged, see value, and be impressed. In most cases, developing context can be a simple matter of making a few declarative statements. These can be non-controversial ideas that most people in the audience will find accurate and provable. The idea is to start an explanation by creating a sense of agreement. We want the audience to feel that they agree with the statements and are confident that the explanation is heading in a direction that they can grasp.

For example, a product manager of a high tech firm may begin her presentation in front of executives with a few statements that frame her ideas and help explain the forest. She introduces the statements with an expectation that what she is about to say is true and something with which the group can agree. Examples may include:

"The web is becoming more social. Forrester research says that . . . "
"More applications are being moved to the cloud. Examples include . . . "
"Video is a growing form of communication on the Web. YouTube has grown by X amount."

When presented effectively, these statements give her audience an invitation that accomplishes a few valuable goals:

- They create a baseline for the talk
- They give her presentation a sense of direction
- They give her audience confidence that her presentation is about something they understand or have an interest in
- They explain the forest

These statements create a sense of context. At this point, she can explain the opportunities, ideas, and questions in the framework of bigger ideas. Her explanation is rooted in ideas upon which everyone has already agreed. As my friend Boris Mann said recently regarding product pitches: "You want to keep everyone's head nodding."

We use these ideas in Common Craft videos. Although they are only three minutes in length, we spend time to build context, usually through these declarative statements.

Our video explaining stock markets is a good example of this.

We approached this video with the idea that stock markets only make sense in the context of a specific kind of business—a public company. We needed to talk about the forest first for this to be an effective explanation. We knew that the viewer needed to see stock markets in the context of bigger ideas. In this case, the video starts with context about the differences between public and privately owned companies:

The numbers we see every business day can tell us important information about our economy; but where do they come from and what do they mean? This is "Stock Markets in Plain English."

Let's get started by talking about companies. There are two basic types. The first is called a private company. Ownership in these companies is private, which means it's not available to everyone. They are usually small to medium-sized, and there are a lot of them, from the bakery down the street to a local trucking company. Private companies are typically owned by an individual or a small group of people. Because ownership is limited, we won't worry about them.

Our focus is on companies that offer ownership to everyone. These are called *public* companies. Here's how they work.

By starting the explanation with a focus on the basic structures of businesses, we can couch the idea of stock markets within the larger idea that there are public and private companies. Only by clearly stating this difference can we ensure that people will see stock markets from the right perspective. The forest of business types helps the trees of stock markets make sense.

Context and Pain

A common story arc includes these basic elements: A character wants or needs something. He or she despairs without it, and must overcome a hurdle to get it. He or she is eventually successful.

In our work at Common Craft we often put this storyline in these terms:

Meet Bob, he has a problem and feels pain
He discovers a solution and tries it
Now he feels happy
Don't you want to feel like Bob?

This framework for storytelling succeeds because it plays to basic human emotions. We all know the pain of wanting something we cannot have—whether it is a mate, an experience, or a product. And likewise, we all know the feeling of satisfaction that comes with overcoming an obstacle.

These ideas also apply to explanations; specifically, to building context into them. For example, an explanation that builds context—not just about the world at large, but how that world impacts and causes pain for someone—can be very compelling. The context then becomes the person's feelings, which can be very powerful.

Example: Google Docs

One of the first custom video projects we completed was for Google Docs, a program that makes it easy to create documents using a website rather than software on your computer. In fact, I used Google Docs to write these very words.

This video was a challenge, not because of Google Docs' features, but because it represented a fundamental change in the way people thought—their mental model—about writing on a computer. Ever since computers became common household electronics, people have used software such as Microsoft Word to write letters and create documents. The document traditionally lived on a single computer. When you needed to send it to someone, you attached it to an e-mail. This mental model is very strong, and few had ever considered an alternative to e-mail attachments.

Then came Google Docs, which accomplished the same basic tasks. You could create a blank document and fill it with anything you needed. You could use bold, italics, and underline. The features most people used were consistent across products. But because Google Docs was web-based, it made new things possible.

We found while writing the script for this video explanation that the features were actually secondary. The first priority was to build context and show how the current home computer-based model was causing *pain*. By beginning with a story of a person sending attachments and uncovering the annoyance it caused, we helped viewers identify with the character. We wanted people to say, "I know that feeling!"

Here is the transcript for the first part of the video:

Home is where we keep the things we need. Whether it's a lawnmower or a coffee pot, it has a home in our lives. Of course, our documents are no different. For years, they've lived on our computers. Each person has their own computer-based home for documents. When we need to share a document, we usually attach it to an e-mail and send it to a friend's or co-worker's computer-home.

Here's the problem: when you attach a document to an e-mail, copies are created. Consider this: if you send an e-mail attachment to three people, the same document will exist in four different places. That's a problem. There's a better way, and it means saying goodbye to messy e-mail attachments.

As you can see, we built context around two ideas:

1. Computers are a home for your documents
2. Your current document home is causing a problem and creating pain

Our goal was to use the first part of the video to show that the standard way of doing things—something everyone does—actually creates problems. This context allowed us to put attachments into a forest of productivity that everyone could see. We wanted them to say, "Of course attachments are a pain, but I never considered how it could be different!"

Working toward this realization allows us to use the rest of the explanation to show how Google Docs creates an online home that prevents all the messiness and pain of attachments.

For the first time, the articles all have a home, a single place for organizing and editing that is accessible from any computer with Internet access. Problem solved.

> Sam is relieved. Without having to deal with attachments, multiple versions, and all that clutter, she can be an editor instead of a document master. For the next newsletter, not a single e-mail attachment is sent, and Sam beats the deadline by a week!

To think about the power of this kind of explanation, consider trying to explain Google Docs by focusing only on the facts and not building context about the pain of e-mail attachments.

- You can create online documents for free
- Invite others to view your document online
- Save your documents online so you can get to them from anywhere

The statements above highlight what makes explanations special. They lack context and an answer to a fundamental question for any explanation: why should I *care*? Used effectively, context helps us answer this question by creating a sense of agreement about the forest. Indeed, it's hard to care about the trees until you've seen the forest.

On the Explanation Scale

As we step through the main elements of explanation in Part II, we'll close each chapter with a look at the explanation scale and where the chapter fits. It's important to understand that our example represents a generic audience starting at the "A" end of the scale. In reality, you may plot your audience in the middle.

As discussed previously, the left side of the scale is often focused on establishing *why*, as in, "why should I care?" This is certainly the case with agreement and context. At this point we're also focused on building audience confidence and helping them feel that the explanation applies to them and is being presented in a way that they can grasp. As such, context and agreement make up our first stepping-stone:

Summary

Too often, we forget the power of building context when we explain ideas. The intimate communication style that helped us earn the respect of our peers and experts in our field is not necessarily a good option outside the bubble of our professions. We must recognize that others experience our explanations differently from outside the bubble. Taking the time to build context means talking first about the forest and then about the trees. Done well, context makes it possible to invite experts and beginners alike to see ideas from a new, helpful perspective.

Next, we'll take another step in the direction of effective explanation by considering how we can use stories to provide a human wrapper for facts.

CHAPTER 7

Story

It should come as no surprise that story is one of the essential elements of explanation. We are surrounded by stories, from TV shows to office gossip. We're innately drawn to them. Stories, however, often take a back seat in professional communications. Although storytelling isn't appropriate in every situation, I believe that storytelling, especially a specific *kind* of storytelling, represents an untapped resource when trying to make ideas easier to understand.

Before we dive in, let's look at how storytelling can change how we communicate facts, offering the audience an alternative way to learn. In the following you'll see two examples, each containing a few sentences about blogs, but in two very different formats:

A blog *is a personal journal published on the World Wide Web consisting of discrete entries (''posts'') typically displayed in reverse chronological order so the most recent post appears first. Blogs are usually the work of a single individual, occasionally of a small group, and often are themed on a single subject.*

—Wikipedia, 2012

and . . .

Meet Allison. She recently created a website where she posts information about her experiences raising a puppy. Her website is an online journal, or blog, where she posts a new entry that appears at the top of her page every few days. This stream of entries has enabled her to connect with dog lovers from around the world.

If you read closely, the two paragraphs above relate the same basic information:

- A blog is a website in the form of an online journal
- Blog entries are organized by time, with the newest entry at the top of the page
- Blogs usually focus on a single subject

The stories above, however, are presented in fundamentally different styles, respectively:

- Fact telling
- Story telling

This chapter's goal is to help you understand each of these formats' roles and recognize opportunities to make the right choice in your explanations.

Stories Versus Facts

We have all grown up with both fact telling and storytelling. For many, these formats are specific to certain locations or situations, and many cases, are mutually exclusive.

Traditionally stories have been told by family members or through books. Facts were the domain of the business or academic worlds, complete with charts and graphs. Indeed, stories in the boardroom may seem as out of place as an income statement for a bedtime story.

This is starting to change, however, and for good reason. We *need* both, and often, we need them together. Stories, in the context of explanations, need facts. And facts can be explained much more effectively in the form of a story. In short:

Facts give stories **substance**.
Stories give facts **meaning**.

Substance and *meaning* are two of the most powerful factors in any explanation. However, we rely on fact telling more than ever and forget the power of storytelling. We focus so tightly on facts that story falls by the wayside—and with it, our ability to give those facts the context and meaning that makes them attractive to our audiences.

Award-winning journalist Al Tompkins wrote:

News writing can be "just the facts" but the difference between fact telling and storytelling is the difference between watching a stock ticker and hearing a story about an elderly woman who lost every dime she needs for shelter and medicine because the market just tanked.

Journalists gather facts and tell stories. No child ever went to bed saying "Daddy read me some facts." It's as if we're prewired to want to hear stories. We want conflict and characters. We want context and resolution. Nobody ever told you the elements of a great story when you were a toddler, but you knew a great story when you heard one.

—Al Tompkins, *Aim for the Heart*, 2

Unfortunately, we have become so familiar with watching the stock ticker in meetings and communications that we assume it's the best way to present information. No matter how much power we know storytelling has, it seems out of place in our professional lives, so we fall back on fact telling.

But I'm Not a Storyteller

I know what you're thinking—because we all have romanticized versions of storytelling in our minds, stories are always filled with emotion and drama. They follow a hero's journey, overcoming huge challenges to vanquish a foe or save a damsel in distress.

Hundreds of story writing books have been written about using this type of story. Although we can certainly learn from them, I want you to forget about this type of story because *explanations do not need to follow the arc of a traditional story.*

However, I do want you to think about the difference between fact telling and storytelling because by recognizing this, you'll also recognize opportunities to present factual information through the lens of a person's experience. This is the story we'll use in explanations—a person's experience.

Let's look again at the two paragraphs about blogs from the beginning of this chapter.

A blog *is a personal journal published on the World Wide Web consisting of discrete entries ("posts") typically displayed in reverse chronological order so the most recent post appears first. Blogs are usually the work of a single individual, occasionally of a small group, and often are themed on a single subject.*

and . . .

Meet Allison. She recently created a website where she posts her experiences in raising a puppy. Her website is an online journal, or blog, and every few days she posts a new entry that appears at the top of her page. This stream of entries lets her connect with dog lovers from around the world.

Notice the difference? This is essentially the same information, in a similar number of words, but the second example is a story. We don't know much about Allison. We have no idea what motivates her, what her challenges or goals are. She is not a well-developed character with emotion and feelings, and there is no drama or conflict in this story. However, we are innately attracted to information in this form. Allison is human, and although we know nothing about her, we can see ourselves in her.

This is the power of story. By adding a person to a narrative, we make the facts more meaningful and interesting. Using people in explanations makes them feel natural and real. Al Tompkins also wrote that "Viewers remember what they feel" (Al Tompkins,

2011). That, of course, is the goal—to create an explanation people remember because it made them *feel* something.

You need not be a storyteller to use stories in explanations. Our focus here is to add a human experience to the presentation of facts. Of course, emotion, conflict, and the other elements that make stories great are welcome, but they are *not required*.

My hope is that this admittedly less-romantic version of storytelling makes using stories in explanations more accessible and appropriate in the professional context. Not only is it easy, the potential is huge.

Common Craft and Stories

Stories have always been an important part of our video explanations at Common Craft and (we have been told) one of the main reasons our videos became popular. When tech-minded people were describing technical features, we were telling stories about people whose lives were improved by technology. One of the most famous examples of this is our video "Wikis in Plain English," published in 2007.

Wikis have been a vexing technology for most people. At heart, they are a type of website that any visitor can edit, which means you can view a web page, see a typo, and correct it yourself. You can even add new sentences and pages. Wikis are simple and have allowed the world to create and grow sites such as Wikipedia. There was a problem, however: the mainstream audience just didn't understand them. Something was missing.

Sachi and I saw that wikis were suffering from an explanation problem. A big reason that they weren't realizing their potential was not related to features, technology, or engineering, but rather to communication. No one was able to explain wikis in a way that helped most people understand and care about the technology. They were all fact telling instead of storytelling.

So we set out to solve this problem by creating a short video that told the story of four people who were trying to plan a camping trip. I originally wrote the story in 2004 and adapted it for video with the goal of helping people see the potential of wikis in their own lives.

These four friends are going on a camping trip. They need to bring the right supplies because they're backpacking. The group needs to plan and plan well, so coordination is crucial.

They're all computer users, so they start planning with an e-mail. It starts with one, but then becomes a barrage. E-mail is not good at coordinating and organizing a group's input. This is the old way—booo! The important information is scattered across everyone's inbox. This isn't coordination!

Let's start over. There is a better way. It requires using a website called a wiki. Using a wiki, the group can coordinate their trip better. This is the new way—yaay!

Most wikis work the same. They make it easy for everyone to change what appears on a webpage with a click of a button. It's as easy as erasing a word and rewriting it.

The buttons are really important. There are two that are essential. They are "edit" and "save," and they are always used together. Let's see them in action.

Here are our camping friends and here is a wiki website. Like all wikis, it has an edit button. Clicking this button transforms the webpage into a document. All you have to do is click it and the webpage becomes a document ready for editing. Editing the page means you can add or remove words or change how they look, just like writing a letter.

Once you're finished editing, you click save and the document becomes a webpage once again, and is ready for the next person to edit it—easy!

Edit—Write—and Save. Using this process, a group can coordinate more easily. Let's apply this to our camping friends, who need to bring the right supplies.

Mary signs up for a wiki site and then sees the new site for the first time. She clicks the edit button to get started. She creates two lists for camping: "what we have" and "what we need." Under "we have" she lists the things she will bring: a cooler, stove, and flashlight. Under "we need" she lists items that others need to bring: compass, lighter, water, and food. She finished the process by clicking save and the website now has lists for the camping trip.

Now it's John's turn. John visits the wiki website and clicks edit, and the page becomes a document ready for him to make changes. John volunteers to bring food and water, so he moves those to the "have" column. He also realizes the group will need a knife and rope. Once he's finished, he clicks save and the wiki is ready for the next person.

Henry visits the wiki, clicks edit and he can edit the page. He remembers they need a tent. Henry saves the page and the wiki is ready for Frank. Frank edits the page and agrees to bring the remaining items, completing the process. Frank saves the page and realizes something awesome. The group has created the perfect camping list — without e-mail — yaay!

But wait! One thing is missing. They need a location for the campsite. The wiki can help with this too, but another page is needed. John visits the wiki and clicks edit to edit the page. He types in the word "locations" and highlights it. He then clicks the "link" button. This changes the word "locations" into a link to a new page.

John clicks save and next, Frank visits the wiki and sees the lists and the link to the new page. He clicks on the "locations" link and arrives at the new page. This new page enables the group to use the same "Edit, Write, Save" process to coordinate locations. This process can be repeated over and over.

These three buttons, edit, save, and link make it possible to organize a great camping trip or create the world's biggest encyclopedia.

Now, this story is obviously not an emotional roller coaster, and it does contain plenty of facts. But the video is about people who have a goal—a well-planned camping trip—and are trying to solve a problem: figuring out who will bring what. Coordination with e-mail is causing them pain; so they immediately see the value of a resource that helps them relieve that pain.

Viewers of this video may not identify with the characters on a personal level, but using a story does allow them to identify with the pain of group coordination and appreciate the value of resolution. Storytelling caused them to see themselves in the characters and feel the satisfaction of a problem solved.

Of course, facts and features play a large and important role in the video, but they are a means to an end, not an end itself, in the context of storytelling. And that's one of the keys to understanding the power of stories in explanations—they turn facts, features and figures into stepping stones that lead to a bigger, more human idea we're wired to understand and remember: the attainment of our goals.

The Simple Ingredient: People

Some of you may be thinking there's no time for stories in your work or that telling a story in a meeting will cause people to roll their eyes. And this *is* a real concern. For many people, stories and storytelling come with an image of a kumbaya moment, when everyone sits cross-legged in a circle and soaks in the words by the light of a fire. As romantic as it may sound, this is not the type of story I want you to imagine, and is probably not one you want to be telling in a professional setting.

Stories in explanations provide a *human wrapper* for ideas. And by wrapping ideas into a relatable story, we can make them appeal to people in a way that the ideas alone cannot.

Consider the wiki script related previously. The characters have no explicit personalities or emotions. We don't know their histories or what led them to decide to camp. All we know is they want to find a productive way to plan a camping trip. In this context, the storytelling comes from the addition of people with needs. By simply adding people to an explanation of wikis, we are able to tell a story of solving a problem that viewers can identify with. All viewers can see themselves in the characters and can envision how a wiki may solve similar problems for them.

Using Stories in Explanation

Once we've completed our research on a Common Craft video explanation, the next step is writing a script. The first version focuses on the big ideas we want to explain and provides the structure for relating those ideas. We are very selective at this point in the process. Because we can only say so much, we decide what ideas are essential and build on them while setting aside others. This is our fact telling version of the script—we're defining the facts we'll explain. Once we feel confident about those facts, we change direction and consider story. We ask ourselves:

- Is this something we can make into a story?
- If so, who is this person and what is their need?
- What is their experience with this subject?
- Will this add to the explanation?

Although not every explanation is fit for a story, we often find that the addition of people and storytelling provides a very useful wrapper for the facts because it gives them boundaries and purpose. Characters help us take the facts and features out of the abstract and apply them to the real world through simple storytelling.

Adding people to an explanation also keeps the focus on the big ideas by limiting what is reasonable. We must present people in explanations with their human limitations. They can't be in two places at once or read *War and Peace* in one sitting. If we explain an idea that involves humans, that explanation is, by design, constrained. This forces us to think in the context of what's reasonable and normal for a person to be able to accomplish.

Therefore, when we approach an explanation with a story in mind, we start to see that characters have limits. A normal person would not use every single feature that a product has to offer, visit 10 stores at a time, or understand trigonometry before algebra. These are constraints that help us make the message more consumable and real. (For more on Constraints see Chapter 11.)

Basic Story Format

Many of the stories we tell in Common Craft videos follow a very simple format that goes something like this, as we've illustrated previously:

- Meet Bob; he's like you
- Bob has a problem that makes him feel bad
- Now Bob found a solution, and he feels good!
- Don't you want to feel like Bob?

You can use this format in your own explanations. To see how, let's look at a story.

Jerome was a 10-year veteran at his company who had recently been put in charge of the machines that make his company's products. This assignment had made him feel a mix of excitement and pressure. Lately, a few of the machines have been showing their age and the employees have voiced some concerns. They were spending more time on maintenance, and safety records were trending downward.

Jerome recently had an engineer inspect the machines and make recommendations. The engineer insisted something needed to change and suggested that the

(continued)

(*continued*)

company invest in more modern—and therefore expensive—machines. Jerome knew this would be a challenge. The executives spent little time on the factory floor, and only a few people in his company understood these complex machines. Although he wasn't used to making a case for spending $50,000, he knew it had to be done. And so he started to prepare.

He decided to create a presentation to explain the machines, what was wrong with them, and what needed to be done to fix them. Within a week he was ready to present, and he decided to start small. He gathered his boss and a few colleagues and presented to them. His presentation was clear and filled with information about the machines and their problems. In tiny font on each slide, he listed every problem he could foresee. From his perspective, the volume of problems would spur the executives to action.

His boss was the first to speak when he was done, and said "I think you've done a great job of capturing the facts of the situation, but I think it's *too* detailed. The executives don't know enough about the machines to appreciate the small problems."

That made sense to Jerome. He could scale back some of the details. Another colleague offered, "You may want to consider what matters to the execs. They're looking for lower costs, higher safety, and happy employees. Maybe there is some way you can make those things clear? Right now it's all getting buried in details." Jerome knew his presentation needed to change, but how?

That night, he was at home reading the newspaper when an idea hit him. His current presentation was all facts and figures, like the financial pages. What he needed was a story—a way to wrap the facts and figures in a way the executives, or anyone else, could easily grasp. He couldn't resist. He dropped the newspaper and started writing the story he wanted to tell.

Over the next week, his story came to life. Although his goal was investment in new machines, his presentation was more about Eva, an employee who ran one of the machines. He used her experiences to show the executives the machine in a new way. It didn't just produce products and data, it was the workspace of a *person*. Eva's story allowed the executives to see how an old machine could have a negative impact on production *and* people. This time around, Jerome could show facts and figures that were grounded in Eva's experiences. By the end, he could clearly connect investment in the machines to an investment in people like Eva, the products she worked hard to produce, and the bottom line.

It was clear after the meeting that he had made an impression. The executives were able to talk about the machines in a way they couldn't before. They could see themselves in Eva's position. Although they remained focused on the facts and figures, the story Jerome told created a wrapper that made the problem and solution easier to understand. Eva's story created constraints that forced him to focus on her machine, its biggest problems, and the consequences those problems had.

Jerome had to cut some of his data and the executives still couldn't describe how exactly those machines worked, but it didn't matter. He traded that for more context and a better understanding of the importance of upgrading the machines. This was the best tradeoff he could imagine because understanding made everything else possible.

As you can see, this example uses the basic storyline we discussed earlier:

- Meet Jerome, he's like you
- Jerome has a problem that makes him feel bad
- Now Jerome found a solution and he feels good!
- Don't you want to feel like Jerome?

When Does Storytelling *Not* Work?

Of course, you may think that storytelling is a panacea after all these positive examples. It's not. Like any of the elements of explanation, stories can be used appropriately and inappropriately.

When a product, idea, or service is inherently human-oriented, it is often a good opportunity to put storytelling into action. An explanation of a social networking website, for example, is perfect for storytelling because it's natural to see it through a person's eyes. Stories have limits, however, and aren't always appropriate for every situation. Here are a few examples:

Process Explanations—Often, explanations are not as focused on revealing big ideas as on working through a process of some sort. In this context, the explanation is often more effectively delivered in the second person perspective. For example, to explain the process of changing a tire, I would ask you to find the jack in truck. Then I would explain how the jack works and where to put it on the truck. Story would simply get in the way in this context. It would do little for you to hear about Jordan's experience changing a tire.

You can see this on the explanation scale, remembering that as you plot an audience on the scale, their needs change as they move toward "Z."

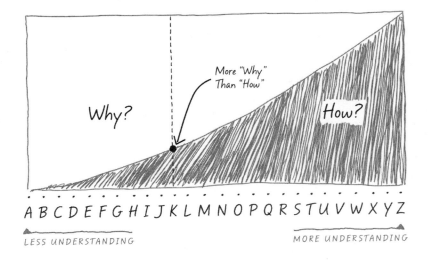

Someone who needs to change a tire already knows the big idea—*why* tire changes are important. This person is likely at "T" on the scale, where he or she is much more interested in *how* to change a tire.

Culture—Every organization has its own culture, and that culture provides clues about the potential for using storytelling in an explanation. You could compare it with using drawings. During an interview I did with *Back of the Napkin* author Dan Roam,

I asked him about situations in which drawings aren't appropriate, and he said to think about it like this:

> *"If you're going to an interview at Goldman Sachs, do you wear a suit? You probably would because the company's culture is known for being buttoned up. But what about an interview at Google? Probably not. The culture is different and being aware of the culture will help you make the right decision."*
>
> —Dan Roam (phone interview April 20, 2012)

Part of your job as an explainer is to understand the culture in which you operate—whether that's inside an organization or as a teacher, salesperson, and so on. Although I advocate using stories as a way to make an idea remarkable, there are some organizations and cultures where it just won't fly, and you need to be aware of this.

Time Limitations—As powerful as stories can be, they take time. We use word-count constraints when working with clients on custom videos. We have to be very clear that we can only say so much in 500 words, which means that we must consider trade-offs. For example, if the client's priority is to explain a large number of ideas and features, we have to make them aware that this requires sacrificing the use of storytelling because we simply don't have the word count to do it all in an understandable way. If your time is limited, storytelling may not be the best use of time.

Personification and Story

As you'd imagine, stories are often a good fit for explanations where the main subject is related to human actions or experiences. These may be customers, employees, historical figures, patients, and so on.

For example, an explanation of space travel could focus on a person's experiences during travel, such as the challenges of operating in zero gravity and the precautions they must take to make it safe. But an explanation of, say, comet formation is fundamentally different. Humans have no involvement or experience with comet formation. As such, it's more difficult to use stories as I've presented them so far. But there is an exception to consider: personification.

What if we could apply human traits to something like a comet? That is *personification*—attributing human traits to inanimate objects. By personifying something like a comet, we can more easily create a story about it. For example, we could follow a "coming of age" scenario where we talk about the comet as if it's an egg that is eventually born into the universe. Big events change its course in life, and so on.

For example, Sachi recently read a book by Sam Kean called *The Disappearing Spoon: And Other True Tales of Madness, Love, and the History of the World from the Periodic Table of Elements.* You can probably tell from the title that the author is using stories to explain and explore the periodic table of elements. But he also uses personification to make complex ideas seem more human and real. Here's an excerpt from a chapter titled "Chemistry Way, Way Below Zero," which focuses in part on lasers. Here's how Kean chose to explain the behavior of electrons in lasers:

> *Inside the laser, a strobe light curls around the neodymium-yttrium crystal and flashes incredibly quickly at incredibly high intensities. This infusion of light excites the electrons in the neodymium and makes them jump way, way higher than normal. To keep with our elevator bit, they might rocket up to the 10th floor. Suffering vertigo, they immediately ride back down to safety of, say, the second floor. Unlike the normal crashes, though, the electrons are so disturbed that they have a breakdown and don't release their excess energy as light; they shake and release it as heat. Also, relieved at being on the safe second floor, they get off the elevator, dawdle, and don't bother hurrying down to the ground floor.*
>
> —Sam Kean, *The Disappearing Spoon*, 287

So here we have a pretty complex process involving lasers and quantum physics. There isn't a traditional story to tell about this particular idea; however, it *is* possible to relate the idea in terms of emotion, desires, and needs. By talking about electrons in the language of a story, it suddenly becomes more human and easier to apply. The normally invisible and emotionless electrons are suddenly riding elevators, feeling sick, having breakdowns, and then feeling safe. It may not be a traditional story, but it does put abstract ideas into a form that feels natural, familiar and attractive to us.

On the Explanation Scale

Having discussed agreement and context, we move into a few elements that are not linear. Although I've chosen to focus on storytelling as the next stepping stone, it is but one option of many for the next step of the explanation. Often, it is effective to build context and then tell a story as the next step.

Summary

We live in a world of facts and fact telling. The idea of using storytelling in explanation is to put facts into a form that involves human experiences, even if we know very little about the humans being described. The simple inclusion of a human or personification can make a huge difference and invite people to see your ideas from a new, more natural perspective. Next we'll explore connections and how they help build on ideas your audience already understands.

CHAPTER 8

Connections

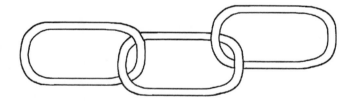

Hollywood moviemakers routinely encounter huge challenges in explaining the movies they want to make. Often, getting a studio interested in and excited about a movie is the first, important step, and it's up to a small team to pitch the movie to them. Studios, however, listen to a seemingly endless stream of pitches, and it takes the right pitch, the right connections, and a bit of luck to get a movie idea produced.

So what's a budding director or screenwriter to do? What approach should one take if given the chance to present a movie idea? How can the team make the movie sound enticing to the studio? Although I don't claim any experience with Hollywood or pitching movies, explanation seems to be essential to a successful pitch. There is an often-told story about an approach to pitching movies that led to a true blockbuster, and it illustrates one of the most important elements of explanation: making connections.

A 1970s filmmaking team was working on an idea that involved a menacing alien. Dan O'Bannon and Ron Shusett worked together on the story and, like most moviemakers, needed a way to pitch it to studios. They pitched the movie using three simple words: "*Jaws* in Space."

The movie *Jaws*, directed by Steven Spielberg, hit the theaters in 1975 and was a huge hit. Millions saw the movie, and even those who did not knew the story. O'Bannon and Shusett, by invoking the *Jaws* name, set the stage for their idea.

Apparently, it worked. Their idea became the Oscar winning movie *Alien*, directed by Sir Ridley Scott and starring Sigourney Weaver. Since its release in 1979, it has made more than $100 million worldwide. Anyone who has seen *Alien* can see that "*Jaws* in Space" was a useful introduction to the big idea of the movie.

Why did it work? Because O'Bannon and Shusett were able to *connect* their idea to something their audience already understood. The studio representatives had likely seen *Jaws* and could use this knowledge to imagine the big idea behind *Alien*. And that's the focus of this chapter—to understand the role of connecting ideas in explanations.

Connecting Your Long Lost Uncle—Old Versus New

If you think about it, many new products or services are simply fresh approaches to old problems. Groupon is a new approach to coupons. Netflix is a new approach to movie rentals. Google Docs is a new approach to word processing. In all of these cases, the new products are built on a foundation that nearly everyone understands. Few people need coupons, movie rentals, or word processing explained to them. Because of this, they provide a great starting point for an explanation. If we can connect an old, easily understood idea to something new, we can help the audience feel confident that they can understand the new idea. Here's an example:

> Let's imagine your uncle Jed recently emerged from the woods after living in a cave for 30 years. The modern world is a mystery for him, and he has many questions. One of the biggest changes he's witnessed is the advent of computers, and he has only begun to learn what they do.

Jed is an intelligent guy, but he has fallen behind the times without exposure to new technology. His years in the cave meant that he missed out on learning about e-mail or websites. Now he's curious and asks you to explain e-mail. Of course, you've used e-mail every day for years; it's become second nature to you. In fact, you've never had to explain e-mail because it's second nature to everyone you know. But Jed is the exception.

You take a few minutes to think about it and quickly find yourself considering the details of e-mail. You think about the format of e-mail addresses, the different e-mail services, and even backend infrastructure such as POP3, IMAP, and SMTP. But you soon realize that these details won't help Jed. These ideas are trees and he needs to see the forest first. To explain e-mail, you need to connect the big idea behind it to something he already knows. If he can understand that, he may start to develop an interest and want to learn more.

Then it hits you. Jed is surely aware of the *postal* service. He's undoubtedly written letters, sent mail, and used a mailbox. More importantly, he knows the value of mail. This serves as a perfect connection for your explanation. To use the previous *Alien* example, e-mail is essentially "letters via computers." This simple idea meant that Jed could connect to the big idea of e-mail enough to feel motivated to learn more.

We often use this connection between old and new in making Common Craft videos because it works. But there's more to it than simply comparing old and new. If you look closely, an element is missing in Jed's story that could make it much more powerful. What we don't see is pain.

You described the postal service without indicating the problems it has. You didn't mention how slow or inconvenient it is, or discuss the cost of postage. These are important points in explanations because they set the stage for a conversation about how the new way can be better, different, and so on. Jed just emerged from a cave, so maybe he doesn't need to see the pain of the postal service. But in most explanations like this, discussing the pain can be an important and useful element.

Notice how the following statements build context regarding the pain in the old way. They're noncontroversial and provide an invitation to come to agreement quickly.

Groupon—We all love to get a discount, but the idea of coupons seems antiquated. They typically appear in newspapers and magazines and are great for things such as shampoo and orange juice. However, when it's time to use them, you hold up the line at the grocery store. But what about coupons for trips to exotic locations or dinner at your favorite restaurants?

Netflix—Few can afford to have a giant library of DVDs, so it makes sense to rent them. But your local movie rental store suffers from a lack of selection and inconvenience. You have to make a trip to the store to rent a DVD and then you find your top choices are sold out.

Google Docs—Have you ever noticed that e-mail attachments cause problems? When you send a document to three people, it means four versions of the document exist and you have to bring all that information together again at the end of a project.

These connections to the old way, presented in terms of pain, set up the new solutions in a clear and understandable way. For example, we made a video on the subject of podcasting, which is a new concept for many people. Instead of introducing podcasting as a new idea, we started the video by talking about something everyone understands: radio.

 Remember the good old days of TV and radio? Everyone would gather around to be entertained. Shows were broadcast at specific times and if you weren't there on time, you missed it—boo! Broadcasts disappeared into the ether. Well, things have changed.
This is "Podcasting in Plain English."
Here's the big idea. Thanks to podcasting, show times don't matter. When a new show is created, podcasting gives you a way to capture it and take it with you to watch or listen to later—usually for free. It makes shows personal and available on demand—that's what makes it different from broadcasting. It works by setting up a connection between a website and a computer, so that new shows automatically show up when available.

This approach gave skeptical viewers a solid starting point by prompting them to connect podcasting to something they already understood and then explaining why that medium is far from perfect. Radio disappears after it is broadcast; this is not a controversial idea. By coming to an agreement about this, we invite viewers to learn how podcasting solves this problem.

Building-on Versus Establishing

The great thing about this type of connection is that it builds on existing knowledge rather than trying to establish a completely a new idea. In the movie example at the chapter's opening, the writers understood that *Alien* was inspired by *Jaws* and used this idea to pitch it. Rather than trying to introduce a completely new idea, they built onto existing knowledge. And you did the same when explaining e-mail to Uncle Jed. *Jaws* in space. Letters via computers. Complicated concepts made simple via connections.

Creating these connections is not a new communication idea; however, it's often forgotten in the context of explanation. When someone asks us to explain something, we may assume it is a new idea to the audience and approach the explanation from the new idea perspective. This can lead us to begin describing the idea via the details rather than looking for connection.

This is often difficult for entrepreneurs who want prospective customers to view their product or service as new and innovative. They want to be able to say that it's not like anything else in the world. Although such products do exist, most products and services live in a world of connections to similar ideas. Ignoring these connections can reduce the potential for understanding a new product because *new* can often mean *difficult to understand.*

However, making connections to related ideas may lead people to make unflattering comparisons. For example, a CEO may not want to connect his new gadget to the Sony Walkman. (Imagine a *Wall Street Journal* headline that says "CEO Says New Gadget Is Like a Sony Walkman.") A marketing professional would bristle at comparing his company's new service to a fast food drive-through or a fax machine. Marketing and public relations teams often strive to *prevent* this from happening. In the context of sales and marketing, getting others to understand an idea often isn't the most pressing priority.

But these connections can be helpful in the context of explanation—when trying to make ideas easy to understand or show why they make sense—because they build on ideas people already know. If explanation is the intent and goal, the benefits of making an idea easy to understand outweigh the potential costs of an unflattering connection. As we will see in Chapter 10, we sometimes have to sacrifice technical accuracy for higher-level understanding to make an explanation work for the audience.

Let's say you find yourself trying to explain cloud formation to a 10-year-old named Jasmine. Jasmine is precocious and never afraid to ask questions. After a visit with her parents, you sit in the yard and she asks you out of nowhere, "Where do clouds come from?"

You smile and your mind races. You have two choices before you: establishing new ideas, or building on ideas Jasmine already understands. Let's look at how this perspective changes your explanation.

Option 1: Explain Clouds by Establishing New Ideas

With this approach, you might assume Jasmine needs to understand the basics of evaporation, condensation, and weather to understand clouds. You would need to introduce some new ideas, such as:

- Clouds form when the water in oceans, lakes, and rivers evaporate
- Clouds are made of tiny droplets of water
- Clouds are part of the atmosphere that surrounds Earth

Option 2: Explain Clouds by Connecting Ideas

With this approach, you would look for ideas Jasmine already understands and use them as a foundation for introducing the big ideas of cloud formation. The question then becomes: what does Jasmine currently understand that could connect her to cloud formation? The answer hits you—boiling water. Jasmine has surely seen her parents boil water and watched the steam rise from the pot. With this in mind, you start at a level that allows her to feel confident. You ask:

[You] *You've seen boiling water, right? What happens when the water gets hot?*
[Jasmine] *It bubbles.* [You] *Yes, that's right. When it bubbles, have you ever noticed the steam that comes from the pot?*

[Jasmine] *Yes.* [You] *When water gets hot it changes and some of it turns into drops that are so tiny they float in the air.*

[Jasmine] *What does this have to do with clouds?* [You] *Well, the steam that rises is like a little cloud. Instead of a pot with water, Earth has oceans, lakes, and rivers. All of that water slowly turns into tiny drops that are lighter than air and when they do, clouds form in the sky. See that one—it's made of tiny drops, just like the drops that come from boiling water.*

Of these two options, which do you think will work best for Jasmine? I predict Option 2. By connecting clouds to something she already knows, we can help her see the big idea and give her confidence from the start that she can understand it. Who knows, this simple explanation could put her on a path to a degree in meteorology.

Analogy

You may have noticed that almost everything we have discussed in this chapter is based on analogy, which compares two ideas for the purpose of outlining a connection between them.

When two ideas connect, they are analogous. In explanation, the use of analogy is a key to making ideas easy to understand. We have already covered a few examples, such as:

- *Alien* is analogous to *Jaws*
- E-mail is analogous to snail mail
- Clouds are analogous to steam from boiling water

Before going too deep, let's tackle one of the more vexing topics related to analogy and something with which I've always struggled: the difference between analogy, metaphor, and simile. Below is my simplified version of the differences between each of these:

Analogies *explain*
Metaphors and similes *highlight*

In explanation, an analogy is an approach to solving a communication problem. They often show a connection between two ideas to make something clear. The emphasis is your intent to make a connection.

Metaphors and similes are different because they are *figures of speech* that connect two unlike things to highlight a point. Here, the emphasis is on the specific word choices.

An example of a metaphor is the phrase, "My classroom is a zoo." This is a metaphor because it compares two unlike things to make a point. The classroom isn't really a zoo, but it makes the point—the classroom is unruly and its members are wild. As a general rule, similes, work in almost the same way, but with the word *like*: "My classroom is *like* a zoo." Again, the emphasis is on the word choice.

Although metaphors and similes may appear in explanations, they are simply a way to phrase words in a sentence. Our focus here is on analogy because it represents an explanation strategy and an approach to connecting ideas.

Common Craft Videos

Connections have always been an important element in Common Craft videos. Although not every video uses an analogy as a connection, many do. Some analogies make up the whole video; others are just a way to make a quick point.

For example, we published a video in 2011 explaining augmented reality, which was a new idea to most people. We chose the topic because augmented reality was becoming mainstream, appearing on smart phones and other devices. The video's goal was to explain both what the big idea was and how it may impact us in the future. Before describing the future, however, or even how augmented reality was currently being used, we wanted to build our audience's confidence. To do so, we needed to connect it to something people already understand.

The truth is, augmented reality has been viable technology for a long time, but few had ever experienced it. However, most have seen what it does in the movies. One example is in the movie *The Terminator*. In some of its scenes, we see the world through the eyes of the Terminator. In that view, a layer of data is transposed over the visual world. This layer shows the Terminator information about what he is observing and helps him identify people by providing information such as their height and identity. His reality is augmented with the layer of data.

Another example is the pilot's view from the cockpit of a fighter jet. The pilot can see the real planes as well as a layer of data about speed, elevation, location, and so on. Again, it's reality—augmented.

It was this second example that we chose to use as a connection to augmented reality for consumers. Here's the script for the beginning of the video:

If you've ever seen a movie with a fighter pilot, you've seen the pilot's view from the cockpit. But something's missing. The pilot needs a layer of information that adds useful items to his view of reality. Recently, this kind of layer started working on your smartphone. But instead of flight data, you have data about the world around you. It's augmented reality.

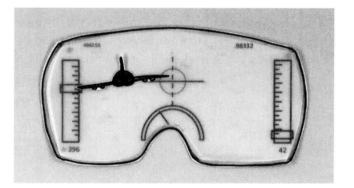

You can see that this analogy allowed us to build on something everyone knows and apply it to a new idea. This explanation took the display that pilots see and made it into something that could appear on a smartphone, but rather than flight data, it shows information about the world around you that comes from the Internet.

On the Explanation Scale

Using connections is another way for us to build others' confidence and lower the cost of figuring something out. Without connections, someone on the left side of the scale could look at something like clouds or augmented reality and see this:

Instead, we want to the audience to see that a connection is simply a stepping stone toward understanding; a small step, like storytelling, that they can take with confidence and at a low cost.

Again, notice that the elements of story and connections in the following scale are at the same level on the scale. This isn't meant to indicate that they are sequential; explanations could use both or just one element at any time.

Summary

We saw by the example of how "*Jaws* in Space" captured the big idea behind the movie *Alien* that connections are one of the most valuable tools in explanation for making ideas easier to understand. The key is focusing on ideas people already comprehend and building on them. If we can give the audience confidence that understanding is easy through connection, we can offer them an invitation to take more steps. It's about saying "You know X, right? Well Y is like it, and here's why . . ."

Next, we'll get a little more specific and take a look at a necessary and useful element of explanation—description.

CHAPTER 9

Description

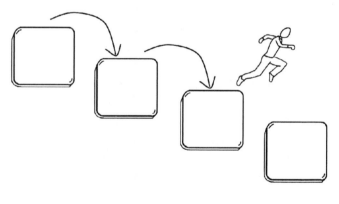

In previous chapters, we focused on elements of explanation that introduce a new idea or explain in a way that helps the audience see it from a new perspective. These elements—context, storytelling, and connections—are most important and appropriate when the audience is near the "A" end of the scale, where they are trying to establish why an idea makes sense and building an understanding of it.

But some explanations must account for people near the other end of the scale, which means approaching explanations from a different perspective.

As a reminder, let's look at the explanation scale with the how/why curve:

As this curve illustrates, someone at "K" may need to see the *why* of an idea more than the *how*. It is important for those individuals to understand that an idea makes sense. Yet someone at "R," who has existing understanding of the big idea, may need explanations that focus more on *how*. This person is more likely to have an informed perspective and need more tactical, detailed information. Consider Andre's team and the early adopters who saw themselves on the "Z" side of the scale. Explanations for this group may need explanations that focus on *how* more than *why*.

For example, a team of mechanics who are learning to use a new tool are unlikely to benefit from a discussion of the importance of repairing cars or from stories about someone using the tool to solve problems. Their level of understanding is near the end of the scale—maybe at "U." Because they already understand the big idea, they need an explanation that focuses more on the details of *how* than *why*.

Another example is someone using a new microwave. They know why the microwave exists and why it makes sense to use one. They may need an explanation of how to get the most out of the machine.

It may seem that we are moving away from explanation to other communication forms such as recipes or instructions. There is some truth to that, and that's not a problem. Explanation is about principles, not rules. It's about intent more than form. It is difficult—nearly impossible, in fact—to draw a line that marks exactly where an explanation begins and ends. Even the most tactical instructions could be an explanation if they make an idea easier to understand. The question simply moves from "Why should I care about this?" to "How can I use this?"

As we'll see in the following, the elements of explanations can still be useful even at the "Z" end of the scale.

Explaining Web Browsers

We published a video in early 2012 that some members of our subscription service called "Web Browsers Explained by Common Craft." We realized while researching the big ideas for this video that it was different from other Common Craft titles. Our videos are often introductions to ideas that may be new to most people, such as search engine optimization. For example, our video explaining QR codes is aimed at people on the "A" end of the scale.

Web browsers are different, however, because they have been so widely adopted. They are preinstalled on almost every new computer, and anyone who has been to a web page has used a browser. Therefore, we felt comfortable assuming that the audience for the video had used a web browser and knew the basic idea and concept. They weren't likely to need an answer to the question "why?"

Initially, we thought the audience might begin at about "G" on the scale. They did not need a high level introduction, but they did require information that explained how to get more out of their web browser. In order to account for the curse of knowledge and poor assumptions, we decided to think about users at "E" and use the beginning of the video to help the audience feel confident about the web browser as a piece of software that every computer has. In this way, we were starting with a connection that builds confidence. Here is an excerpt from the script:

When you use a computer, software makes it easy to write letters, edit photos, and watch a video. The same is true when you connect a computer to the Web. Software makes web pages useful and easy to navigate. This software is called a web browser.

Because the concept of the browser is likely clear, we started to account for more tactical items—the actions one must take to use a browser:

> You open a browser with a click, and it connects you to web pages using web addresses, or URLs. You simply type an address in the address bar or click a link on a web page, and your browser uses the address to find the right page.
>
> Computers and mobile devices come with browsers automatically, but you can also download new ones for free, and even have more than one on a computer.

At this point, we had built a basic platform designed to help the viewer feel confident. We introduced (or reviewed, depending on each person's level of understanding) the idea that web browsers are software that automatically come on computers to make it possible to view websites.

Now it was time to think about how we could walk the viewer through the powerful tools and options in the most common web browsers. Of course, like other software, there are multiple ways to do almost everything in a web browser. Part of learning to maximize a browser requires knowing how to find and execute the features. Therefore, we spent some time introducing parts of the browser that we would reference later in visual form:

> But browsers do a lot more. To explore the options, we'll use menus like this and keyboard shortcuts, which make things happen by pressing two buttons at the same time.

Again, this was a stepping stone headed toward a full explanation. Next, it was time to dive in and show the viewer specific tools and features that are important for getting the most out of web browsers.

> For example, with billions of web pages and long addresses, it can be hard to keep track of what's important to you. A browser can help by remembering where you've been over the short term [by allowing you to use] the back button, or [help you] over time with the history menu. And you can add a bookmark for any page to get back to it quickly.

And a browser is a little like a vehicle—you can customize it to make it your own. Instead of new wheels and a stereo, you can add browser add-ons or extensions. You can download these from your browser's website and plug them right into your browser with a click. But your browser does a lot without extensions.

For example, you may need to see three websites at the same time for comparing movie times. Instead of opening three browsers, you can just open new tabs in a single browser window. As long as tabs are turned on, you can add new tabs from the browser or with shortcuts.

And what would you do without search? Thankfully, most browsers come with a search box built-in. Just enter a keyword here and your browser will take you directly to the results.

Browsers also make remembering passwords easy. When you enter a password, your browser can remember it for the next visit. But be careful, using this feature on shared computers is like giving strangers your car keys.

Oh, and here's a great shortcut. If you're looking at a long page of travel info and only care about Hawaii, your browser can search the page. Just ''find'' it using the ''edit'' menu or the keyboard shortcut and those words will be highlighted on the page.

And finally, you need to update browsers regularly. Be sure to install updates when asked. This will keep your browsing safe and sound.

A web browser is your window to the online world and knowing what's possible can make it work for you.

So there it was—web browsers explained. Although we may not have used a character to tell a story or created a vivid connection that dominated the video, the principles of explanation were still at work.

We spent a few sentences on context by establishing that we were referring to software on a computer. We used a quick connection to explain the idea of a browser extension by transforming the concept of tabs into a short story about movie times. Then we wrapped it up with a reminder about the browser being a window to the online world. We were still using the principles of explanation, but the elements were more compressed and focused.

To make this clearer, let's contrast this explanation with a recipe.

Explanation Is Not a Recipe

We all depend on recipes from time-to-time—and I don't just mean the kind for cooking. From baking a cake to changing a tire to installing software, recipes give us direct and specific actions that will produce the desired outcome. They have been tested and documented. No other information is needed in these scenarios because recipes are designed for almost anyone to be able to follow, regardless of their level of knowledge. They are designed to exist without context.

For example, let's consider our web browsers' example in the context of a recipe. We could have approached it like this:

Ingredients

- Computer with web browser
- Internet connection

Web Browser Use

- Start computer, open web browser software
- Type URL in address bar to visit website
- Open bookmarks menu in toolbar, bookmark current website
- Visit browser website, download extensions for extra features
- Click File → New Tab to open new tabs in one browser window

I think you get the point.

Could a recipe for using a Web browser be effective? It could help, and its accuracy and efficiency may even make it preferable to some. However, the recipe is missing elements that make an explanation more powerful—a focus on packaging ideas and on answering the question, "Why?" The video explanation doesn't just tell you how to open tabs; it explains *why* you would want to open tabs. It doesn't just tell you how to use the "Find" tool; it invites you to do so by providing an example of when you would want to use it.

What if recipes operated a little differently?

Pick up almost any cookbook and you'll see nicely formatted recipes that produce amazing dishes. Each ingredient, measurement, and step is exhibited in an easy-to-read and consistent format. For example, a recipe for bread is likely to call for baking powder, and a beer recipe is likely to call for hops. If you follow the recipe perfectly, you will have the expected outcome.

But what if you knew *why* the recipe requires these ingredients? What if you had more information about hops and why they are part of beer in the first place? What if you understood how hops impacted bitterness and balanced the sweetness of the barley in beer? And what if you had information that would allow you to customize the recipe based on your preferences? This would open up a world of possibilities and allow you to see why you should care about hops and want to learn more. This is the difference between a recipe and an explanation: a recipe tells you *how* to do something; an explanation does as well, but it also tells you *why* it makes sense.

On The Explanation Scale

Descriptions are a valid and normal part of explanations and are best used toward the "Z" end of the scale, where the priority is likely to be more focused on *how* than on *why*. As you can see in the following, descriptions are likely to be more appropriate as we move toward the "Z" end of the scale.

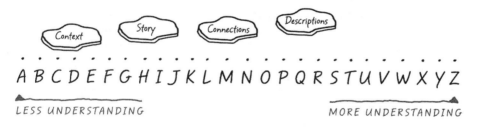

Summary

Explanations come in all shapes and sizes. Perhaps the most powerful form of explanation makes a new, complex idea easy for people to understand and care about. But explanation can be powerful in many other situations. When people already feel comfortable with a concept, they may need a different kind of explanation—one that focuses on *how* more than *why*. These are situations in which we may be prone to falling back on a recipe approach and focusing solely on the specific tasks that will produce the desired outcome. In some situations, this may be appropriate. By thinking about these steps in terms of explanation, however, we may see opportunities to present the ideas in a form that interests the audience and motivates them to learn more. This may mean building context, making quick connections, and using short stories to show not just *how* to complete a task, but *why* the task makes sense.

Next we'll move away from specific stepping stones and into more general ideas that apply to explanations of all types, starting with the basics of simplification.

EXPLANATION AT WORK: JERRY JACO, K-8 TEACHER

Jerry Jaco is a K-8 school teacher who also teaches professional development classes. He uses multiple types of explanations and is a big believer in the power of video.

Jaco explains, "I typically use video presentations throughout the year, both those I create myself as well as those I can acquire from other sources. I have found that coupling a live stream of simple but compelling images with a succinct voice-over, as demonstrated so well in the Common Craft style, is an effective way for my students to retain the ideas that are presented.

"Research indicates that when a student both sees and hears the information at once, the brain is more likely to retain it because the brain is processing on two different channels in parallel. Many instructors impart educational information in traditional settings by overloading one channel versus the other, to the detriment of retention. Furthermore, providing another channel of information alongside the difficult one makes perfect sense to assist those students who struggle with language, or who have visual impairments.

"Another way I use video explanations is as a component of my teaching websites. Again, when you put a lot of verbal (i.e., written) explanation on a site, most people glaze over and then skip what you're trying to get across. However, putting the key elements into a succinct video is much likelier to benefit students—mainly because they're more likely to actually spend the time viewing it."

Jaco also sees explanation as an excellent way to engage students in complex and sometimes confusing subjects such as intellectual property rights.

"One critical area of knowledge I need all my students, both adults and young people, to understand is connected with intellectual property and copyright laws. This has some very serious implications for teachers in particular, but everyone needs to have a general awareness of the issues involved. Video explanations help me lay out the information in a way that students can easily apply to their own work."

In regard to the outcomes he expects from explanations, Jaco is a believer in the power of video to help students retain information. Further, Jaco voices his belief—which is a big part of this book's message—that being remarkable is a big asset.

"The key ingredient is also a fundamental principle of any presentation; the content must be compelling, and therefore memorable. In creating such presentations, one cannot rely simply on the conventional or cliché renderings of words and images. The creator must seek the most elegant phrases and imagery to convey the material as effectively as possible. Otherwise, the audience will not take note of the content as informative and interesting, but more likely will see it as the same old stuff revisited."

CHAPTER 10

Simplification

We've discussed how we all suffer from the curse of knowledge to some degree, in one area or another. One of the most profound products of the curse is the inability to simplify. Although valuable, the knowledge we bring to the table inhibits our ability to predict what will appear simple for others, which then makes our explanations overly complex.

To illustrate this point, consider the concept in computer software called *virtualization*. Most computer users are not familiar with the term and have no need to know it. The people who *do* understand virtualization are often those who work in the computer industry or who take a keen interest in computers; let's call them geeks. This sets up a classic situation in explanation.

We have the geeks at the "Z" end of the scale and the average computer user at the "A" end.

Because this book is about moving people from "A" to "Z," we will zoom in a bit more and consider the role of simplification in this situation.

From the geek perspective, virtualization is a big, complex subject. To understand it, you'd need to be able to grasp several different ideas about software and operating systems. It seems impossible to explain these concepts to a novice computer user because there are so many details and ideas that are prerequisites for understanding virtualization. For them, it looks like this, with numerous ideas, exceptions, and details:

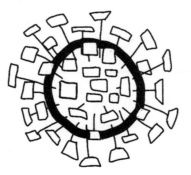

When an idea seems this unattainable, it has an impact on how experts explain the idea. The curse causes explanations to be:

- Accurate, yet incomprehensible
- Detailed to the point of being ineffective
- Filled with unfamiliar words
- Presented without context or application

However, when we consider simplification, we focus on transforming that complex bundle of details into big, understandable ideas that serve as stepping-stones to future understanding.

This is a perfect time for those who already understand virtualization to set guidelines. If you, as an expert, seriously want to help novice users understand concepts like this, you must think a little differently, which means you . . .

- **Do not make assumptions** about what people already know
- Use the **most basic language** possible
- Zoom out and try to see the subject from the **broadest perspective possible**
- **Forget the details** and exceptions and focus on big ideas
- **Trade accuracy for understanding**
- Connect the basic ideas to **ideas the audience already understands**

Inside that big bundle of details and ideas is a single notion that will make the overall concept easier to understand. To get to that core, you can use the aforementioned guidelines like a machete to hack away at all the extraneous knowledge that causes complexity. Soon enough, you will find any complex idea can be made simple. It just takes a new approach.

Meet Steve. Steve has been in the computer industry for years. These days, he's in the business of selling software to big companies, and he's good at it. He knows the details of the software, but he also has a playful personality that attracts people to him. Lately, his company has been selling virtualization software, and he knows more about it than almost anyone at his company. Most days, he's on the phone or at a customer site, singing the praises of virtualization with the IT team and the CIO. They all live in the IT bubble and speak a language that's uniquely technical. This has become second nature for Steve.

Recently, Steve and his family joined cousins at a family reunion and repeatedly had the same conversation. Then, however, he was cornered by his aunt Martha,

(continued)

(*continued*)

who had many questions. She recently bought a computer and has become fascinated with how they work. Not content with small talk, Martha quickly moved into the details of his job. She said "I know you're in the computer industry, but what do you *really* do?"

Steve said he "sells software."

"What kind of software?"

"It's called *virtualization software*." Usually at this point, he expected people to tune out, but not Martha.

"What's virtualization?" she asked. Steve was stunned. How could he possibly answer that question in the middle of a family reunion? Did she even know what an operating system is? He looked for a way out.

In Steve's mind, virtualization was impossibly complex. It took him months to get his head around it himself, and hardly anyone at work knew as much as he. Because he's never tried to simplify it for someone like Martha, he abandoned the effort by telling her that "it's really complex software that's hard to explain." With that, he leaves her standing by the pool, icy beverage in hand.

Later that night, Steve tossed and turned. His interaction with Martha bothered him. He had left her standing there with no answers. Not only was it rude, it showed that he had lost the ability to think about virtualization from a novice's point of view. He resolved that night to solve this problem. His goal was to explain virtualization simply for someone like Martha.

It was all he could think about the next day, so much so that he blocked off his calendar at the end of the week to focus solely on it. As time passed, he started to notice the language he and his colleagues routinely used and thought about Martha. For the first time, he could see that although she was the focus, the goal of simplification could have a positive impact on his work.

Eventually, he invited one of his peers to help simplify virtualization with him. What could he have said to answer Martha's question that would have helped her?

They started with a discussion about what Martha likely already understood about computers, and made the following list:

- She has a computer and is familiar with software programs
- Her computer has an operating system such as Windows or Mac OS
- She knows that computers have limited resources, such as memory
- She knows that businesses use computers

They also considered language. What words or phrases did they use every day that were likely to sound foreign to her? They listed things such as:

- Virtualization
- Servers
- Platform
- Utility computing
- Processing power
- IT

The next step was to zoom out. Steve and his friend needed to see virtualization from a high level. To do this, they considered why virtualization exists:

- Computers are expensive and need to be maximized
- Virtualization uses computer power more efficiently
- Virtualization reduces waste
- Virtualization increases flexibility
- Virtualization saves money

Now it was time to focus. They needed to boil down everything they knew about virtualization into a few big ideas. This was a challenge because they both had such deep knowledge of the subject. Steve's friend started by asking about which kind of virtualization would be their focus. Platform? Hardware? Desktop? Software? Steve took a deep breath. Figuring this out was a challenge.

(continued)

(continued)

They both agreed that the *type* of virtualization didn't matter for Martha. It was a detail that may have stood in their way in the past, but now that Steve was serious about solving this problem, he knew he had to stay focused on the big picture. He must keep in mind that Martha just needed a simple idea.

Soon enough they began to tackle the concept and underlying core of virtualization. They knew that if they could help Martha see the overall concept, she could make sense of the details. Steve had an idea—what if they focused on virtualization on her computer? If she could understand it there, he could build on that knowledge and connect it with how businesses use it.

Steve's friend balked and waved his hand. "It's apples and oranges. The virtualization on *her* computer is not what you're selling."

Steve reminded him that Martha needed to see the *concept*. "For it to make sense, we must forget the details and stay focused on the big ideas. Otherwise, she'll never get it."

For the first time, Steve began to picture it all coming together. He would use Martha's computer to relate the concept of virtualization and then slowly expand the idea to businesses and connect it to his job.

The next weekend Steve asked his wife for Martha's phone number and she chuckled. "You and Martha have a lot in common these days?"

He smiled and said "After today, she will understand my job."

His wife chuckled again and said "Good, maybe she can help me get it!"

Steve made the call and confessed to Martha that her question had been on his mind for a long time. He apologized for not being able to offer her better answers, and let her know that he was now calling to make up for it. Martha was taken aback. She never imagined he would be so considerate and helpful.

Steve was ready for the challenge. He took great care to speak in terms she could understand. Here's what he said:

"Martha, you have a computer, right? If I'm not mistaken, your operating system is Windows." She confirmed. "Well, that computer has all sorts of powerful tools inside that make it work. When you use your computer, you typically only use part of what it can do. You're actually not even using most of that power. In fact, it's going to waste. My job is to sell software that makes use of that extra power on computers. This way, you'd have Windows, plus another system on the same computer, one that's dedicated to putting that extra power to use without impacting you. It's like having two computers in one. Does that make sense?"

Martha got it. She could imagine her computer being more powerful than she needed, and could see that it was wasteful. She could also envision her computer having room for another system to use that computing power. She wanted him to continue, "Why would I want to add another system to my computer?"

He laughed and said "Good question—let's look at how this idea could be used . . .

"*Your* computer is the only computer in your house. However, many businesses have hundreds, even thousands of computers, including huge, powerful ones. Just like your own, these computers also have extra power that these organizations could put to use. This is a lot of potential power across a big company. The software I sell makes it possible for the company to use that existing power instead of buying and maintaining more computers. That saves them money, and helps me send the kids to college."

Martha was both speechless and satisfied. It all made perfect sense, and she now understood enough about virtualization to explain it to her friends.

But for Steve, it was just the beginning. This exercise in simplification changed his perspective and helped him see that although most of his colleagues might have known about virtualization, they had no idea how to explain it to those who didn't. Now that he had figured out how to make the idea accessible to people outside their bubble, both his marketing team and his CEO wanted to hear his explanation so they could help people like Martha see the big idea.

Steve was able to simplify the complex idea of virtualization by following a few guidelines:

- **Do not make assumptions about what people already know**.

  He gauged his audience's level of understanding and listed the pertinent subjects they were likely to understand.

- **Use the most basic language possible**.

  He considered his normal language and listed what words, such as *virtualization*, *servers*, and *platform,* would *not* sound familiar to his audience.

- **Zoom out and try to see the subject from the broadest perspective possible**.

  He wrote down statements that reflected the basic ideas of virtualization, such as the fact that computers have extra power that goes to waste and how software can make use of that power.

- **Forget the details and exceptions and focus on big ideas**.

  He chose not to discuss the types of virtualization or even use the word *virtualization* until the end.

- **Be willing to trade accuracy for understanding**.

  He related virtualization to Martha's computer, even though his software would never work for her.

- **Connect the basic ideas to ideas the audience understands**.

  He used her computer as the starting point for understanding virtualization.

The idea at the core of virtualization was rather simple: virtualization puts unused computer power to work. For someone like Martha, this was a graspable idea and one that could be built upon.

Steve realized that his years of experience had led him to see virtualization as a big, complex bundle of ideas. Understanding it required an understanding of IT, computer infrastructure, operating systems, and computer science. But he found that all the details, exceptions, and ideas were just noise—and barriers to understanding—for someone like Martha. To get to the core, he had to eliminate the noise until only the simplest idea remained and could be heard.

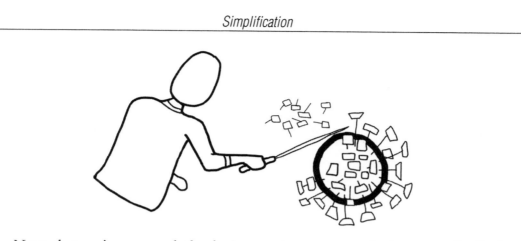

Now that we've covered the basic stepping stones and elements of effective explanation, it's time to get more specific and work towards putting these ideas into action. But first, we'll talk about constraints, which are a way to approach the process that helps bring focus to our explanations and account for our audience's needs.

CHAPTER 11

Constraints

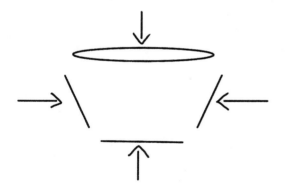

Before getting into the nitty-gritty of creating an explanation, I think it is important to consider one of the most powerful tools we have to turn ideas into easy-to-understand explanations: constraints.

Living in a world of amazing abundance seems like it should make our lives easier, but does it always? We have multiple places to enjoy dinner, more apps than we can possibly download, and detergents of all sizes and colors to keep our clothes clean. But this abundance comes with a cost. So many choices can cause us to feel overwhelmed and lose confidence that we can make the right one. Crafting explanations can seem overwhelming in a similar way. We are faced with so many choices that we can easily feel frustrated. As we'll see in the following, constraints are what will help us feel confident and capable of making the right choices.

Psychologist Barry Schwartz wrote about this phenomenon is his book **Paradox of Choice**, in which he cites multiple studies that show that too much choice often leads to unhappiness, and can even cause a person not to make a decision at all (Barry Schwartz, 2003). One particular study, called "When Choice is Demotivating," showed that increasing the number of choices had a negative impact. From the book:

> *One study was set in a gourmet food store in an upscale community where, on weekends, the owners commonly set up sample tables of new items. When researchers set up a display featuring a line of exotic, high quality jams, customers who came by could taste samples, and were given a coupon for a dollar off if they bought a jar. In one condition of the study, six varieties of jam were available for tasting. In another 24 varieties were available. In both cases, the entire set of 24 varieties was available for purchase. The large array attracted more people to the table for tasting, though in both cases people tasted about the same number of jams on average. When it came to buying, however, a huge difference became evident. Thirty percent of the people exposed to the small array of jams actually bought a jar; only 3 percent of those exposed to the large array of jams did so.*

So, as much as we think we *want* a large number of choices, too many can become a problem and prevent us from feeling happy with any choice.

We encounter this same decision making process when we're thinking through explanations. Our myriad choices can seem overwhelming and prevent us from feeling confident that we choose the correct analogy or story, for instance.

Consider the seemingly simple example of buying men's ties. If you have ever been to a shop that specializes in ties, then you know that it can be overwhelming. A tie is a simple article of clothing, but it comes in an incredible variety of colors, fabrics, patterns, and shapes. We may think that walking into a tie shop with every option on the table would be liberating. We believe that seeing every possible alternative will allow us the freedom to experiment and give us options that we may have otherwise missed. It's a logical way to think about selecting a tie.

But is the same true for crafting explanations? When we have ideas for an explanation and need to give it more definition, do we want to consider every possible option as a starting point? I believe the answer is no, and to show why, let's revisit the tie shop example.

Let's say that you decide you will limit your choices before you visit the tie shop. You only want a tie that is dark green and has a simple design. This changes how you think about ties. Suddenly, what was once an overwhelming selection becomes more defined and useful. Deciding on a specific color and design will allow you to approach the process with focus and confidence that the right decision is possible.

What you've done here is introduced a set of constraints to your process. Before you even started the decision making process, you defined and limited your options to a couple of variables, and in doing so, you narrowed an overwhelming selection to a manageable number. In this way you are not liberated by endless choice, but rather by constraints. By intentionally restricting what is possible, we have the potential to highlight factors that might have otherwise been hidden. It could be that by focusing only on simple, dark green ties, we see a color combination that becomes the basis for a new look. Constraints bring focus and attention to things that may have been overlooked otherwise.

Common Craft and Constraints

Since creating the first Common Craft video, we've worked under a very specific set of constraints that give our videos a specific shape, form, and intent. Examples include:

- **Project duration**—all video projects must be complete by a certain date
- **Video duration**—the video must be so many minutes long
- **Ideas**—only so many ideas can be explained in those minutes
- **Format**—we can only do what is possible in Common Craft style
- **Language**—we must present it in the vernacular of a specific audience
- **Music**—we do not use music in Common Craft videos

By agreeing on a set of constraints, we can start to evaluate ideas from the context of what is possible within them. If a video must be under 3 minutes, this constraint gives the explanation a very specific shape. You can only say so much in 3 minutes. By only making videos in Common Craft style, we are constrained by what is possible with paper cut-outs and markers. And having project deadlines forces us to keep the project moving.

Although these constraints limit, they also liberate. We intentionally create a container that allows us to evaluate what's in or out quickly, which frees up our attention to focus on other things.

Consider the Common Craft style constraint. Because we only work with paper cut-outs and a whiteboard, we don't need to think about live-action footage, motion graphics, or any other format; it doesn't fit in our container. The same is true with music. By not adding music, we don't spend time choosing the right music or requesting permission to use what we want. It simply isn't part of our consideration. By limiting these decisions, we can use our time to focus more specifically on what does fit into the container—what matters to our project.

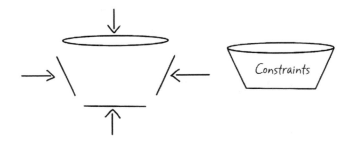

In fact, there is real science behind this idea. Author and speaker Jonah Lehrer, who recently published a book on creativity called *Imagine: How Creativity Works,* wrote an article for *Wired* magazine called "Need to Create? Get a Constraint" on this subject.

In the article, he writes about a study conducted by Janina Marguc at the University of Amsterdam and published in *The Journal of Personality and Social Psychology* that seems to support the idea that constraints allow us to think more freely.

The larger lesson is that the brain is a neural tangle of near infinite possibility, which means that it spends a lot of time and energy choosing what not to notice. As a result, creativity is traded away for efficiency; we think in literal prose, not symbolist poetry. And this is why constraints are so important: It's not until we encounter an unexpected hindrance—a challenge we can't easily resolve—that the chains of cognition are loosened, giving us newfound access to the weird connections simmering in the unconscious.

When all data and ideas are on the table, there is endless potential, and we could spend weeks working through it in an effort to explain it all. Constraints help us eliminate most of that data and focus on connecting what will fit within our constraints.

For us, constraints give an explanation form and shape. For example, information on the audience is helpful when thinking about ways to present an explanation, but the audience is only a starting point. To build and present an effective explanation, we need to think through a number of questions that help us see the explanation in the context of constraints.

Constraints and Your Explanations

You will likely find explanation problems that need to be solved in your professional life—situations in which initially every idea and option to solve it is on the table. Perhaps you know the subject so well that you're not sure where to begin, and you need to give your explanation a shape to move forward. One way to do this is to think about the explanation in terms of constraints and eliminate all the ideas and data blocking your view. You can start by using the constraints that we encounter in making a video:

- **Timeline**—when do you need to have the explanation ready?
- **Duration**—how long should it take to explain?
- **Location**—where will the explanation be presented?
- **Format**—how will the information be presented?
- **Idea volume**—how many ideas can you explain in the defined duration?
- **Language**—how technical is the language that the target audience speaks?

For example, determining that the explanation needs to be ready in one week, should take three minutes to explain, is covering two ideas, is presented via a slideshow presentation, and will be written in the language of an executive would be a great start. These are constraints at work, and by defining them, you can see new opportunities, connections, and considerations that you didn't see before.

Of course, these constraints are more like guidelines than rules. They give the explanation form, but are not requirements in most cases. They simply help you give scope to the explanation.

A common process for brainstorming and organizing ideas is to use sticky notes, each of which contain one idea. You can think about all the themes and ideas that could be a part of your explanation, and then put them all up on a wall.

Next you'll organize them into groups and start filtering them by removing the ones that don't fit with the big idea groups that emerge. In her book *Resonate,* presentation pro Nancy Duarte describes the filtering process in terms of "murdering your darlings":

Although you may feel that all the ideas you generated are insightfully riveting and took a ton of time to generate, they need to be sorted and organized—and some ideas need to be killed off.

Filtering is very important. If you don't filter your presentation, the audience will respond negatively—because you're making them work too hard to discern the most important pieces.

One of the best guides for this process is to think about the constraints of your explanation outlined previously. After all, there are only so many ideas that will fit if your explanation needs to be ready in one week, take three minutes to explain, cover two ideas, be presented via a slideshow presentation, and be written in the language of an executive. You have to take the other ideas behind the shed and murder them. That's the perilous life of an idea.

Summary

It seems paradoxical that constraints liberate, but I believe it's true. Only by considering a specific situation's limitations can we identify the right combination of factors that work to achieve the outcomes we want. Often, it is through restrictions such as duration, language, audience, and format that we can discover new ideas and opportunities to make our explanations remarkable.

We've covered a lot of ideas to this point. You've seen the stepping stones for moving people from "A" to "Z" on the explanation scale. We've discussed simplification and constraints as ways to give our explanations a defined form and shape. Next we'll bring all these ideas together in the form of a written explanation, which allows us to think through and organize our ideas for maximum effect.

CHAPTER 12

Preparing for and Writing an Explanation

Think for a minute about your favorite scene from a movie, your favorite speech, or your favorite cartoon from your childhood. You might remember watching Yoda teach Luke to use the Force in *Star Wars*, live footage of Martin Luther King, Jr. in Washington, D.C., or the colorful cartoon artwork that presented Wile E. Coyote's constant quest to stop the Road Runner.

Although different, these experiences all have one important element in common: they were all born and developed with the written word. In fact, most of your favorite movies, TV shows, comedy sketches, speeches, cartoons, and performances all begin in the form of words. The world of entertainment depends on writers to turn ideas into scripts that can be used to communicate a particular show's vision. This is certainly the case with every Common Craft video. The script is how we work through ideas and create a vision for every explanation.

Writing is a logical step in the process of transforming an idea into something useful, as it is for explanation. The best path to solving explanation problems and making ideas easier to understand is to have explanations in writing, where they can evolve before being presented. Like screenplays for films, written explanations become living documents that provide a means for sharing and developing ideas and concepts. Although explanations may be presented in text form and be effective, it is the *process* of writing that clarifies an explanation and gives it a form that can be presented in many ways.

The Common Craft Writing Process

Common Craft is recognized for the paper-and-whiteboard visual style in our videos. Known to many as the Common Craft style, this is how people experience and remember our work. At first glance, it may seem that the visuals are what makes the videos work, as if the heart of the explanation lies in the artwork or the representation of ideas on the whiteboard. But from our perspective, nothing could be further from the truth. At our core, we are writers. Our explanations' value arises from a deliberate and rigorous focus on writing scripts for each video. The images on the whiteboard are simply visual aids for a carefully crafted script.

Of course, the visual elements are a critical portion of our work, and they make our work remarkable. In fact, we have often evaluated our work in terms of separating the script from the visuals. Our goal is for both of them to be useful on their own, without the other element accompanying them. In other words, a script (or voice-over) should be effective without visuals and the visuals should be effective without a script. By making this a priority, we can amplify the power of both by combining them in a single experience.

Our focus before any presentation mode, however, is writing. Whether they are custom productions for clients or ready-made videos for our library, all Common Craft videos follow the same basic process prior to the storyboard phase:

1. Big idea—We are going to make a video about X.
2. Research and discovery—What main points do we need to make?
3. Script writing—How will we make it easy to understand?

Big Ideas

Every video project starts as an idea based on a number of inputs. This is simplified if we are hired to make a video; the client usually comes to us with specific goals. The majority of our work, however, is focused on video titles *we* decide to pursue. We always look for the potential to fill a gap, to create an explanation where none exists or where one exists in less usable forms. For instance, we published a video during the writing of this book called "Twitter for Business." It was based on a gap that we saw about the options businesses have to use Twitter as a business tool. This video was aimed at businesspeople who are looking for ways to use Twitter to reach business goals and also at the public, who wonder why so many businesses suddenly have a Twitter account. These initial decisions are important because they represent a long-term investment. If we decide to make a video, we are deciding to invest significant time and effort to make it happen.

Your situation is likely very similar. If you intend to solve explanation problems, it is essential that you identify the right problem or big idea. These problems take many forms, from internal communications to home page design, and part of the explainer's job is to recognize when an explanation could offer a solution. Imagine talking to a product manager and saying "I think we need to focus on explanation here. People just don't understand the product's value." Or telling an executive, "Before you share this news, let's think about it in terms of explanation." These are examples of opportunities to identify a big idea that could be explained.

To get started, scan the environment of your work or home and look for explanation problems. Where are ideas not being adopted because of poor communication? Look for gaps in understanding that, if filled, would give people a way to see a big idea from a new perspective. If you keep a list of these, you'll start to see that the world is filled with opportunities for better explanations.

Research and Discovery

Like most explanations, Common Craft videos do not focus on presenting new facts so much as packaging existing facts into new, more understandable forms. This means that our research and discovery is not only focused on the facts themselves, but on how they have been communicated or explained in the past. Subject matter experts can point you to existing examples and help you validate your assumptions. Our goal, however, is to identify a big idea, get to the facts about it quickly, and pay attention to the existing explanations, all in an attempt to identify a *remarkable* approach to solving the problem.

For example, one of our most popular videos is an explanation of social media. This video was one of our most difficult to write because social media is an amorphous, constantly changing idea that means different things to different people. Because our business strategy (as well as my previous consulting experience) has always been built on social media, the facts and definitions were clear to us. We identified a problem related to existing explanations, which all seemed to focus on the *how* of Social Media. They explored various tools and features, yet none answered the *why*—as in, why should I care? Why is this social media thing such a big deal? Why is this going to change my life?

This discovery of the lack of *why* gave us direction. We knew that our explanation would not focus on defining social media or discussing tools and features; instead, we would fill the gap that existed by answering *why*. To do this, we told a story about a town that learned to make its own ice cream (which is a thinly veiled allegory of the democratization of media). The residents of the town and the big ice cream company saw the results of everyone's participation in the ice cream business and how it created positive change. I feel confident that no one has ever seen a social media explanation like this one.

Here's part of the transcript:

 Let's take a visit to Scoopville, a town that's famous for ice cream. For over 20 years, Big Ice Cream Company has been making high-quality ice cream with a big factory in town. A few years back, the company did focus groups and found out that they could maximize profits by offering three flavors: chocolate, vanilla, and strawberry.

The residents of the town were content. They never thought it could be different. Then something happened in Scoopville—a new invention came to town. Suddenly, everyone could make their own ice cream for only a few dollars. This changed everything.

The Smiths decided to make pineapple ice cream. The Jones' made ice cream with pecans. Soon, every kind of ice cream imaginable was being made by Scoopville's residents at very little cost.

Of course, some ice cream was more popular than others and that was okay. Sylvia's pickle ice cream had a very small but loyal following. That was fine. She only needed enough income to buy ingredients for her next batch. Jarret's red velvet ice cream became so famous, he created his own store. Over time, people started to think differently about ice cream.

It didn't always come from a factory. It also came from friends and neighbors. It became something to share, something to bring people together, something to celebrate. Big Ice Cream Company still made the best vanilla around, and to their surprise, demand even grew. But it was the unique, original, and authentic flavors made by the residents that brought people to Scoopville.

The big ideas for you might be new concepts or existing ideas that you feel have been limited by their current explanations. As such, your job in research and discovery is not to simply uncover the facts, but to understand the way those facts were communicated in the past. Approaching the research in this broad way will increase your chances of identifying major points and finding ways to make your explanations more useful and remarkable.

Now that we have defined and documented the problem we want to solve and reviewed how the ideas were communicated in the past, we can begin writing a first version of the script.

Script Writing

The script is the foundation of any explanation. Although it may not be the medium you ultimately use to present it, it represents the heart—the touchstone from which everything else emerges. So far, you've read about packaging ideas into explanations that include context, connections, stories, and descriptions. The script is where these ideas come to life and begin to take shape.

I want to touch on the issue of constraints before going further because constraints give scripts form and direction. They are an essential part of designing our Common Craft video scripts because we often work within word count limits. Our videos are always under four minutes long and we use a rule of thumb that dictates that one minute of video time is about 150 words for my voice-overs. This means that 600 words is the upper limit of word count for any Common Craft video. In reality, we generally shoot for 500 words or less.

Knowing this limitation informs the design of the script. As you can imagine, you can only say so much in 500 words; therefore, the constraint has an impact. It's essential to think ahead about duration in approaching your script. Do you need this idea to be understandable in a specific amount of time? Sixty seconds? Four minutes? If so, it's important make this part of the scriptwriting process.

Following is an example that can serve as a guide to structuring explanation based on best practices from Common Craft videos. I want to stress that it is not a *formula*, by any means; there are no specific rules in explanation. Master screenwriter Robert McKee said as much in his award-winning book *Story*, which begins with these points in the Introduction:

> *Story is about principles, not rules. A rule says "You must do it this way." A principle says, "This works . . . and has through all remembered time." The difference is crucial. Your work needn't be modeled after a "well-made" play; rather it must be well-made within the principles that shape our art. Anxious, inexperienced writers obey rules, unschooled writers break rules. Artists master the form.*
>
> *. . .*
>
> *Story is about eternal, universal forms, not formulas.*
>
> *All notions of paradigms and foolproof story models for commercial success are nonsense. Despite trends, remakes and sequels, when we survey the totality of Hollywood film, we find an astounding variety of story designs, but no prototype.*

It's in this spirit that I provide a sample outline for scripting explanations. The template is based on dozens of Common Craft videos. It's a very common form in our work, one that works for us and our goals.

As you know, building confidence in your audience is key to moving them down the scale, one stepping stone at a time, from *why* to *how*.

Here's an overview of the elements of a basic script, in order.

- Agreement
- Context—problem/pain and vision of solution

- Story
- Connection
- Description
- Realization of solution—how
- Call to action

Agreement. These are noncontroversial statements that start to frame the explanation's direction. They could be formulated by starting each statement with "We can all agree," as in, "We can all agree that sales are down over last year" or "We can all agree that digital storage prices have continued to fall in recent years." By making these statements, we give the audience easily graspable and understood information.

Context—Problem/pain and vision of solution. Explanations are well-suited to reveal why an idea makes sense. One way we can do that is to state, in clear terms, a real problem that everyone understands. There is a problem and it's painful.

"When sales go down, we're forced to make difficult choices and think hard about how we spend money."

"With storage prices falling, we're missing a big opportunity to rethink how we invest in our infrastructure."

Next, we present a vision for the future. These are often *what if* statements that inspire the audience to imagine a world in which this problem has been solved.

"What if a new product line could change this number for next year?"

"What if we could save enough money to make our reach goal for next year?"

The explanation has been very general up to this point, and the ideas and language have built confidence and context. Now the audience is likely looking for an answer—what will solve this problem and achieve this vision of the future?

Because every situation is different, the next step in our process is never consistent. The goal is the same in whatever form the explanation takes, however: we want to present an idea in the most understandable way possible for a specific audience. We use the following elements in doing so:

1. **Story**—Introduce a character and outline some basic facts about this character. (Hint: the character is likeable and very similar to the audience.) This character lives in the world we introduced earlier and feels the pain. It's a bad feeling. This

character then discovers a new way to do things (the big idea). The character tries it, it feels better, and it makes sense (how it works). The character feels satisfied because life has changed for the better. *Samuel was losing sleep because his new product was off-schedule, but now that he's using XYZ product, he's able see the light at the end of the tunnel.*

2. **Connection**—The idea here is to take an indirect approach to addressing the big idea. Rather than addressing it outright, we talk about something like it in the form of, "You know X works, right? Well, Y is a lot like it in these ways." These connections help the audience see the big idea without getting bogged down in details. The connection is about understanding the concept. *Samuel started to see that XYZ was kind of like an assembly line for fixing his product. Each step was automated and kept the process moving.*

3. **Description**—Sometimes explanations take the form of more tactical introductions about how to accomplish a specific task. Often, these are most appropriate when the audience is on the right side of the explanation scale. *All Samuel had to do was follow a simple process to start the job.*

Of course, you can mix and match these elements as needed. For example, you could tell a story about someone who learned to see an idea through a unique analogy.

Realization. Now that we've shown the idea at work and given the audience a new perspective, we can show them the outcome: how the idea will change lives or actually works. *Now Samuel is getting all the sleep he needs because he knows XYZ is there to keep the project on track.*

Call to Action. Finally, we wrap the explanation up with an invitation to take an action. In Common Craft videos, it's often a summons to learn more. It could also be an invitation to contact someone, complete a form, sign up for a class, or try out a product or service. This marks the end of the explanation. *To learn more about how XYZ can help your company stay on track, go to this website.*

The Real Thing

Now that we've walked through the structure of a basic script, let's see how it can look in the real world. In the following I have included a transcript from a Common Craft video about BitTorrent that reflects these elements:

AGREEMENT AND CONTEXT

 Our computer files aren't like they used to be. These days, a short HD video can be over a gigabyte in size. That's *huge*. And the problem is that the bigger they are, the harder they are to share. Thankfully, we have options that make sharing big files over the Internet fast and easy. This is "BitTorrent Explained by Common Craft."

Story Begins

Blake was so excited. He's the president of his local Sasquatch fan club and recently heard that a new video was circulating. He couldn't rest until he had the video on his computer.

Problem/Pain

He tried to download it from the original website, but it was painfully slow. Because so many fans were trying to download it at the same time, the website crashed. He was discouraged.

Vision of the Future

Then a fellow fan said the video could also be downloaded via BitTorrent. She said that unlike typical downloads, files using BitTorrent actually download faster when more people are involved—and it works with any kind of file.

Connection

To see for himself, Blake downloaded BitTorrent for free from bittorrent.com. He opened the program, and was a little confused. There were no videos and he wasn't sure where to start. But soon he realized that's because BitTorrent is a little like a web browser. Just like a browser needs websites to be useful, BitTorrent needs special files called *torrents* to work.

Story

A quick web search pointed him to websites with torrents galore. Soon enough he found the Sasquatch video torrent, downloaded the torrent file to his computer, and with a simple click, BitTorrent immediately sprang to action and the file started downloading. He could see it was

(continued)

(*continued*)

working and he wondered how. Later, his friend made it clear by talking about how downloads typically work without BitTorrent.

When someone downloads a file, it comes to their computer in a stream from a single source. When multiple people want the file, that single source can get overworked and can even shut down. BitTorrent solves this problem by making each downloader a source. This allows them to get pieces of the file, but also provide pieces to each other. Together, the downloaders become a network of multiple sources — all working to provide pieces to one another. This is what makes downloads fast.

Description

A couple of things behind the scenes can make this happen. First, Blake received .torrent file when he clicked "Download". This file has all the information about the video file, like what pieces are needed to complete it; however, something is missing. Blake needs a way to connect to others who have the pieces he needs for his file. BitTorrent uses a computer called a *tracker* that helps Blake's computer find other computers called *peers*. The tracker keeps track of computers that are downloading or already have the whole file, and introduces Blake's computer to them.

With the connections in place, Blake receives what he needs and also distributes pieces to others who are downloading as well.

Realization of Solution

Blake got it. BitTorrent works because it turns downloaders into sources — and more downloaders leads to more sources and faster downloads.

In the end, Blake's video downloaded in no time at all. But he was a little disappointed — what he thought was a Sasquatch was only a Wookie. But at least he now knows that BitTorrent is a faster, easier way to download files from the Internet.

The secret to crafting a great explanation is not necessarily using the right formula, it's learning to recognize when people can't grasp an idea and developing a script that solves the problem.

To make these ideas more clear, we'll take a look at an example in our next chapter that follows a team through the process of learning about and writing an explanation.

CHAPTER 13

Bringing an Explanation Together

Meet Emma, a human resources manager of a large clothing retailer. Her company is in the middle of a big change: they're transitioning every employee to a new benefits system with a high deductible health plan. Emma is heading up the team that's been charged with communicating this change to employees.

Although Emma has a great relationship with her colleagues, she's also nervous about this new program. She knows the details of the transition and can see it will be a positive change for almost everyone, but she's not sure how to ease this transition for the employees. Her goal, as outlined by the CEO, is to have 50% of all employees sign up for the new plan within six months.

After dozens of meetings with her team, they are finally ready for the rollout. They've crafted a set of e-mails that will serve as an introduction and invitation to join the new plan. The team agrees that the employees will want to know how it works, so they provide a couple of short paragraphs to explain the plan.

Dear Valued Employee,

Our company has a new health plan that will help us manage our health-care expenses and may lower your monthly health-care expenses. It's called the high deductible health plan. Here's how it works:

Your monthly premiums are likely to decrease and your deductible will increase from $500 to $1,000 when the new plan is implemented. This may help decrease your overall health-care expenses because deductibles are only paid when health-care services are used. If you and your family don't use health-care services, you won't pay deductibles at all, which means your overall expense is likely to decrease.

Emma gritted her teeth and clicked send on the e-mail designed to make the new plan easy to understand. And then . . . crickets.

She wasn't sure what to do. There were no questions or comments for the first few days, and to make matters worse, no one signed up for the new plan. Feeling puzzled, she assembled her team to assess the situation. Some members had done some reconnaissance work and discovered some useful but disappointing information: people didn't understand the change and didn't care about learning more. Some didn't know what a deductible was or why it mattered.

Despite her best efforts, she felt like a failure. Emma knew she needed a new path forward. What could she do?

When her team gathered the next week, one member named Carlos introduced an idea. He had been learning about explanation and informed the team they had a classic explanation problem. The new plan was beneficial, but people were not adopting it because of how it was being communicated. Carlos told them that it's a common problem and there are ways to plan and execute better explanations.

This idea took Emma by surprise. She had never thought about the new program as an explanation, much less considered how to improve it. She asked Carlos to come to the next meeting with a communication plan.

Carlos took the challenge and arrived at the next meeting with a few big ideas to set the stage. His goal was to help them see the potential of explanation as a communication strategy that could solve their problem.

To start, he asked the team about the last time they explained an idea, any idea, and used that to point out that we all take explanation for granted. As he said, "We do it all the time without giving it a thought. But what if we *did* think about it? What if we could improve our explanation skills? Do you think it would have a positive impact?" The team was intrigued; this had never occurred to them. Carlos could see the lightbulbs turning on and relished the proud smile from Emma. Everyone agreed: it was time to think differently about explanation, with Carlos as their guide. He and Emma hatched a plan for him to research and present his idea in a few days.

Soon Carlos realized a funny thing about teaching people about explanation—he had to walk the talk. He needed to *explain* explanation. Thankfully, he had started correctly by helping people come to an agreement on the potential of explanation. Everyone was on the same page; he just needed to take it a step further and ensure everyone understood exactly what an explanation is. This would help him build the team's confidence.

When the day finally arrived, Carlos began his presentation by making some factual statements. He stood at the whiteboard and wrote a few, including:

- Health care is expensive and costs are rising
- The company helps employees manage their health-care expenses
- The current health-care plan will change
- The new health-care plan is a high deductible health plan
- High deductible health plans help employees manage expenses better

Everyone agreed that these statements were accurate and noncontroversial. In fact, they were the messages that every employee saw in the recent e-mail. Carlos then used these facts to distill the essence of explanation. He said, "The key idea about explanation is that it describes facts. These statements on the whiteboard are facts, and our goal is to describe them in a way that makes them more useful and easier for our colleagues to understand. And we'll do that by taking a step back and thinking about how to package them in a way that appeals to our audience."

Carlos continued, "If we do it well, our communications will make people care about this new plan, and that's part of our goal. If we can make people care, they will become more motivated to pay attention and look more closely at the details. They will become customers of the ideas we're communicating."

At this point Emma jumped in. "That makes sense, but it's a very tall order. Can we really expect people to care about a health-care plan policy change?" Carlos agreed it was a challenge, but he asked her to reserve judgment for a bit.

He had one other important point to make about explanation before moving on: "At the core of nearly every explanation is a simple question: *why*? Explanations may also cover *who, what, where, when,* and *how,* but the core question to answer is: *why* does this idea make sense?" Carlos then went to the board and added a simple word to each fact to set the stage:

- Health care is expensive and costs are rising—why?
- The company helps employees manage their health-care expenses—why?
- The current health-care plan will change—why?
- The new health-care plan is a high deductible health plan—why?
- High deductible health plans help employees manage expenses better—why?

These questions will help them frame their explanation.

"Now," he continued, "it's time to think about the audience and identify the problems that keep our current communications from being effective." Carlos then introduced two ideas for this:

- Explanation problems
- The curse of knowledge

He started with a quick discussion about explanation problems and used technology as an example. He asked the team if they used a couple of popular online services. Most didn't, but they were familiar enough with the services to understand where he was headed.

He then asked them, "How could these services enhance interest in using them? Through better engineering, better design, or a lower price?" These didn't really matter. "What about usefulness? Would it help if they were more useful to you?" Maybe, the group mused, but it would depend on purpose because they didn't know how to use the products in the first place.

"Exactly! These products have an explanation problem. Their adoption is limited by how they are being communicated. Being well-designed, potentially useful, and free is great; but unless the product can be explained, it's difficult for people to care about it enough to try it."

He quickly connected this idea to the project at hand. "Our new health-care plan has an explanation problem, too. Despite being a good policy and a positive change for employees, adoption will be limited unless we can explain it better."

The pieces were starting to come together. The team could see that something had to change and that the idea of better explanations made sense. But how? What could they do to improve their explanations?

Carlos proposed the first step to better explanations is to understand what makes them such a challenge, and for this, he introduced the curse of knowledge. Instead of diving in, however, he took a step back by asking the group: "Have you ever talked to someone who was very informed in a particular field—someone like a doctor, stockbroker, or mechanic—and felt like they were talking to you using another language? Did it seem like you needed a translator to understand?" Groans were heard around the room. Everyone knew the feeling.

"That's the curse of knowledge at work. These people are so steeped in their knowledge—they know so much about that particular field, be it medicine or finances or cars—that they've lost the ability to imagine what it's like *not* to know. Their language sounds natural to them and their peers, so they assume everyone else understands, but unfortunately, they don't. The curse prevents them from altering their language to account for different audiences. And we all suffer from the curse in some way. Everyone sitting in this meeting has the curse of knowledge for HR subjects. Therefore, to give better explanations for those outside of our department, we will have to keep our language in-check."

To make his point, Carlos headed to the whiteboard and drew a simple scale from "A" to "Z." He wrote "Less Understanding" on the "A" side and "More Understanding" on the "Z" side.

ABCDEFGHIJKLMNOPQRSTUVWXYZ

LESS UNDERSTANDING   MORE UNDERSTANDING

Carlos said, "This is the Explanation Scale, which we can use to help us think about our explanations. Right now, this team is at the 'Z' end of the scale. We know the new plan very well. The company's employees are at the 'A' end of the scale. They don't have a strong understanding of the new plan.

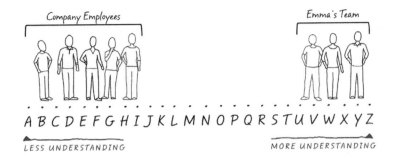

"Our goal is to create explanations that move them to the right—toward the 'Z' end of the scale."

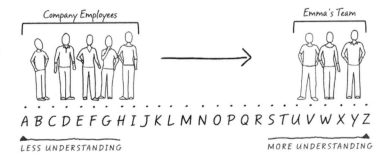

"One reason it's not working well now is because we're all so far on the right end of the scale. It's hard for us to imagine what it's like not to know about the new plan. We're forced to make assumptions about their existing knowledge, which influences how we communicate. It could be that we assume we're reaching everyone, when our communications are only reaching to those at the 'G' level—leaving most employees in the dark."

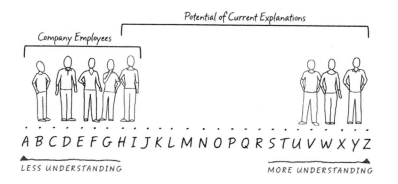

This affected Emma, who couldn't stop thinking about the e-mail she sent weeks before. What assumptions was she making about the employees, and where would that message appear on the scale? Could the curse have caused her to miss the mark in her communications?

The goal became clear for the team: to create an explanation that accounted for everyone on the scale and to use explanations to move them to the right. But the big question still remained: *how*? How could they create an explanation that did just that?

Fortunately, Carlos was ready to answer that question. He referred back to the explanation scale to make a quick point. "Here's one way to think about the needs of people at different points on the scale." He drew a simple dividing line and added two words—*why* and *how,* like this:

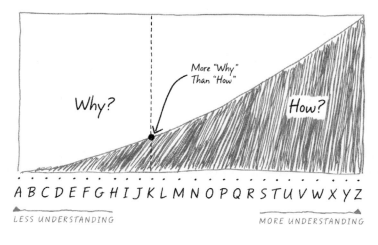

He described how he could plot the team's approach to explanation on this curve, with the idea that explanations need a combination of both *why* and *how*. For example, someone at "C" needs more information about *why* the new plan makes sense. Someone at "R" is probably informed enough to understand why, however, and needs more specific information on *how* it works.

Carlos connected this idea to the statements he wrote on the board at the beginning of the meeting by saying, "Imagine someone at the 'A' end of the scale and think about the facts we discussed previously. This person needs to see the why before the how. And just like we discussed, it's a simple matter of describing the facts by asking the question: *why* does it make sense that it works this way?"

- Health care is expensive and costs are rising—why?
- The company helps employees manage their health-care expenses—why?
- The current health-care plan will change—why?
- The new health-care plan is a high deductible health plan—why?
- High deductible health plans help employees manage expenses better—why?

After everyone reconvened after lunch, Carlos drew the following simple picture on the explanation scale and asked the team to think about the new policy from this person's perspective:

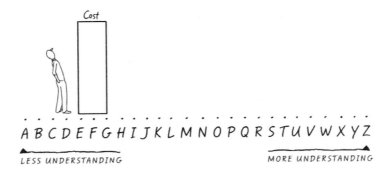

He explained how the new policy appeared from an average employee's perspective: "Think about how this change looks to an employee. It's big and unwieldy. It takes time to understand, and our colleagues have more pressing things to do during a busy day. The cost of figuring out the new plan is high for them; and since they can't afford the investment, they tune out." The team nodded in agreement.

He then turned to the problem's solution and said, "That's why we have to offer them an invitation to learn that helps them feel confident and provides stepping stones to learning more. What if we could present the new plan so that instead of seeming monolithic, it seemed more like this?"

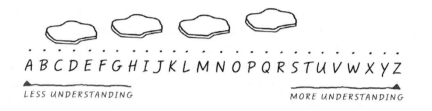

A B C D E F G H I J K L M N O P Q R S T U V W X Y Z

LESS UNDERSTANDING   MORE UNDERSTANDING

Suddenly, the path forward became clear. Their explanation would be organized by steps, leading the person from the "A" side of the scale to the "Z" side.

Emma wasn't completely convinced, however, and had a question. "I think this makes sense, especially for people who know very little. However, a good percentage of our employees are actually toward the middle of the scale. Aren't they going to be turned off by all the introductory information?" It was a good point: this approach did appear to focus only on the beginners.

But Carlos was prepared and able to help her see it differently. "It's true that this approach does account for people at 'A' who have very little understanding; but we must start there to capture every employee. And yes, this means that those in the middle of the scale will hear about information they already know. But the question becomes: would you trade one for another? Does it make sense to orient the start of the explanation at 'L,' knowing a group of beginners will be left behind, or start at 'A,' knowing people in the middle will find it a review?" Emma thought about that for a minute.

Carlos put the question in a different context. "Think about it in terms of cost. What costs more, leaving beginners behind, or reminding the informed?" *That* made sense to Emma. An explanation that starts at "A" will simply validate the ideas of those who already know the subject and give them a bit more confidence in it. But the cost of starting beginners at "L" is very high because those at the left end of the scale are cut out completely. Only by starting at "A" could they help everyone feel confident.

The group felt satisfied and ready to move on. They understood the underlying concept: they needed to account for people at "A" on the scale and to provide stepping stones to move them to the right. But what were these stones?

Carlos could feel his excitement building as he went on. "This is where an explanation really comes together and where we have to think creatively. There are many ideas we can provide as stepping stones, and the right combination is different for every situation. There is no specific formula; it's more of an art.

"And thankfully," he continued, "getting started is easy. Our goal is to invite those at the 'A' end of the scale to feel confident, which requires us to build context. This will help them see the big picture, and then the details will make more sense to them. We want them to understand the forest first and then the trees.

"Let's say we pick an important part of the new plan, such as coverage for family members. You could say this is a tree. It's important and helps the person understand a single idea. But that tree becomes much more valuable if we take time to talk about the forest first. It's part of a bigger picture and so allows the person to see the tree in the context of all the other ideas—the forest."

Emma recalled the e-mail about the plan she had sent and concluded that it was essentially a set of trees—ideas that existed without context or foundation.

"We can start to build context by making a few statements that are factual and not controversial. We want everyone to be able to feel confident. We could even frame this as *we-can-all-agree statements*." Carlos provided some examples.

We can all agree that . . .

- Health care is expensive and costs are rising
- Health-care coverage is an important part of being financially responsible
- The company needs employees to be happy and healthy
- The company needs to help control costs for both employees and the company

"As you can see, these statements accomplish a few things. First, they create an easy initial step that can be understood with confidence without complex terminology. Second, they frame the direction of the explanation: it's about health-care plan costs, something that impacts everyone. Third, it creates a foundation for future ideas and/or goals. We're starting to build the forest.''

The team was excited about piecing together this communication puzzle.

"Next we'll focus a bit more and present a big idea. For now, let's say it's something like: *To help ensure everyone's health-care expenses are manageable in the future, we're switching to a new plan called the high deductible health plan—and this message will help you understand what that means.*"

He continued, "As you can see, here we've focused on the big idea and assured our colleagues that our intent is to make it easy to understand. We've given more context and therefore more confidence. Note that we're still at the 'A' end of the scale, with the priority focused on the question *why*; we'll get to *how* later. The question we need to keep in mind is '*why* does this make sense?'"

Carlos then challenged the team to brainstorm the answers to this question. Why does it make sense that the new plan will help employees manage health-care expenses in the future?

After some discussion, a few big ideas emerged. The best one came from a mid-level manager who described the situation as follows: "With the old plan, people were paying for health-care whether they used it or not. This new plan means they can save money because cost is connected to use. Your costs can go down if your family is healthy, and that couldn't happen before."

This claim elicited some emotional reactions. The health-care plan manager immediately shot back "That's an oversimplification; it's true for some, but not for everyone. There are a number of important exceptions and I'm not sure we want to set that expectation." Everyone could see that she had a point, including Carlos. But he was prepared for this argument.

"I think you make a valid point. However, it's crucial for us to make the overall concept absolutely clear. We're still talking about the forest and we want people to feel confident. We'll talk about the exceptions and details in a bit; but our goal for now is to be certain that the big idea is clear for people. Otherwise, the details won't make sense."

They decided to stick with a very similar statement: *Up to this point, your monthly health-care expense was constant, whether you saw a doctor or not. This new plan means that your health-care expense may change based on your family's use of health-care services. When you and your family are healthy, your monthly expense can potentially decrease.*

From Carlos' perspective, the explanation was on the right track. The group was able to recognize that the big hairy idea of the new plan was too overwhelming to discuss at first. They had to get to its core and make the value easily visible. Although some team members had valid concerns, they were slowly becoming oriented to this approach.

As a reminder, Carlos went back to the whiteboard and illustrated the progress so far. He estimated that they were at about "J" already.

The forest was in place and it was now time to introduce some of the trees and make some choices about what stones to use. Carlos pointed to the scale.

"So far so good. We've accounted for those who had no understanding and now they can see the big picture of what we're communicating and why. We're now at about 'J,' and our next step is to head toward specificity. But first, we need to make some choices about the next stepping stones. There are a number of options we could consider at this point; we could even combine a few of them."

He continued, "The two most common options are to tell a story or make a connection—and we can do both. Connections are often analogies that connect a new idea to something the person already understands. Stories follow a person's experience in learning about and trying a product or service."

"From my experience, connections are a great starting point if the big idea still isn't clear." Emma was pleased.

Carlos encouraged everyone to come up with ideas that were not related to health care but that operated like the new plan. They had to be common concepts with which everyone was likely to be familiar. "The idea here is to say 'you know how this works, right? Well this plan is very similar to it.'"

A team member tried to clarify. "So we're saying that the old plan was a subscription with a constant price and new plan is also a subscription, but costs less when it's not used, right? Maybe we can think about things that come with subscriptions or memberships? Maybe newspapers and magazines? What about health club memberships?''

When the team got too concerned with details, Carlos reminded the group that the connection has to make sense; however, it can operate with an unrealistic assumption to make a point.

"For example," he pointed out, "the magazine concept could work. Let's say that you have a magazine subscription that you paid for every month whether you read it or not. But now the magazine publisher offers a new plan where you pay less if you don't read very much of it.'' Carlos recognized that it was a clumsy example. "I understand it's not realistic, and would never happen. But does that matter? If it makes our point and helps people feel confident, I think it should be considered. The question is, does this connection help people see the big idea of the new plan in a clear and accurate way?''

The team was split. They decided to go ahead and draft the idea with the recognition that it may be edited or removed.

Here's one way to think about the new plan. Let's imagine that you subscribe to a magazine. Some issues you read from cover-to-cover; others go straight to the recycling bin. Under this system, you're paying for issues that you don't use. Now let's consider a new plan in which the magazine's price is based on usage. You still pay a subscription fee, but that fee decreases in months when you don't read it. This way, you can save money when you don't use it. Our new plan is similar. It's built around the idea that your expenses should decrease when your family is healthy. It just makes sense.

Carlos then suggested that they use a story. The team looked skeptical and Carlos smiled. He had seen this coming because he had the same reaction when he first heard about stories in explanations. To help get everyone oriented, he explained that stories take many forms. Some are very developed and complex, but others, like the kind the group will use, are much simpler and become a way of relating facts in a form that makes them more meaningful.

Carlos said, "By simply adding a person's experience to a set of facts, we can create an experience that appeals to people and informs them without an extraneous backstory. Think of it this way: instead of fact telling, we'll be storytelling.'' The team still wasn't convinced, so he provided an example.

Carlos walked across the room, grabbed a stapler and said, "Let's talk about the facts of this stapler. It's made of metal. When pressed, it produces a staple. Staples can be used to connect pieces of paper. Staplers are common office supplies." He continued, "This is fact telling; I'm sharing some useful facts about staplers."

"Now let's talk about storytelling, which takes the facts and packages them into a different form. For example . . . meet Marvin, an office worker. His job fills his desk with papers that he often misplaces. But now that he has a common office stapler, he can organize the papers by stapling them together with one easy press. This simple metal device helps him be more efficient and impress his boss."

The team got it. They didn't need to know Marvin's backstory or career goals, or follow him through a set of challenges. All they needed was to see the stapler through Marvin's experience.

Before diving into the story, the team talked about what it should cover and decided that it could be powerful to show how two different people may experience the new plan. This would allow them to provide a little more detail. They decided to describe a family who is healthy and saves on health-care expenses, compared with another family who needs to see doctors more often. With Carlos as their guide, these stories took shape . . .

To see how the new plan may impact your family, meet the Smiths and Johnsons. These two families have a few things in common. Both have two children and a parent employed by our company. They even live in the same neighborhood. Both families need health insurance, and, like everyone else, have seen costs rise over the years.

The Smith family has been very lucky. The children rarely fall ill and only visit the doctor for annual physicals. Mrs. Smith has had her insurance premiums go up over the years and felt that, although insurance was necessary, it was a little unbalanced because her family didn't use much health care.

The Johnsons were not as lucky. One family member has a chronic illness and they rely on health insurance to make care affordable. They hate to see premiums rise, but it's better than paying out-of-pocket because this would cause them to go into major debt.

Now that the company has a new health plan, both families want to understand what it will mean for them. Apparently, monthly premiums will decrease and deductibles will increase. They can both see that it's a balance—that savings on a monthly basis may go to deductibles if they see a doctor.

Mrs. Smith feels good about the plan because if her family's good health continues, her premiums will reflect less usage. Although the cost may be higher when they do see a doctor, they can put away the savings in premiums each month and possibly have this extra money by the end of the year.

Mr. Jones is also happy to see lower monthly premiums. The deductible may be higher, but he realizes that his family needs more care than most. And because the coverage isn't changing, he can continue to depend on the insurance.

As you can see, the change in health-care expenses with the new plan will depend on each employee's health-care needs. The result is a new balance of higher deductibles and lower premiums, one that creates a money-saving opportunity for many families. And, it helps ensure that the company can also afford to offer a plan that makes sense for all employees.

The team was excited as they finished this exercise. They'd managed to bring the new plan's boring policies to life through a story. They couldn't imagine trying to use fact telling to communicate with employees when this approach made so much more sense.

The pieces were starting to fit together. Not only was the team thinking differently about explanation; they now had a solid start on an explanation strategy. They had a way to make a connection to an idea everyone knows well and a story that makes the facts more understandable and usable.

As a final exercise, the team needed to think about how these ideas would be presented. Could it be accomplished through e-mail? What about a presentation? Could they make a simple video or visual of some sort?

Carlos asked Emma for a few days to get prepared to answer these questions.

PART 3

Present

It's a tragedy when the product of a presenter's preparation and effort is compromised; not by the content of their work, but by how it's presented. For example, a playwright's work could be compromised by poor acting, a brand's message could be compromised by ineffective advertising, or a scientist's discovery could be compromised by incomprehensible writing.

All of these ideas' potential value is hindered by their *presentation*—the highly important point at which the ideas move from behind the curtain into the real world. This isn't an easy transition, and it comes with risk. It requires skills and approaches that may not come naturally to those who created the original work. Playwrights are not often directors and scientists are not always writers. An amazing idea, poorly presented, loses value quickly.

And so it is with explanation. Explanations cannot survive in isolation. They must be skillfully promoted and shared to achieve their potential. To create change and solve problems, they must move from behind the curtain in a form that fits with the audience's needs. Even the most amazing explanation loses value quickly if presented poorly.

This is the focus in this part of the book—to move from packaging and writing explanations to releasing them into the real world in a form that engages the target audience and helps them feel confident. My goal is to not only help you consider your presentation options, but also to introduce the potential of tools, ideas, and approaches you may not have considered before. In the end, your explanations should be remarkable—not only because they solve explanation problems, but also because you've presented them in a way that makes people notice them.

In the following chapters, we'll cover:

- The lessons that we at Common Craft have learned in presenting multimedia explanations
- How to think about media choices and use constraints to find the right ones
- Different types of visuals, and how to use visual thinking in your explanations
- How Emma's team approached the options to present their explanation

To finish up, we'll zoom out and think broadly about your life as an explainer and the potential to make explanation a productive part of your organization's culture. We'll also explore various opportunities to use explanations through real-world case studies and examples that highlight explanations at work.

CHAPTER 14

Common Craft's Lessons Learned

People often ask us what makes Common Craft video explanations work. What is it about them that engages people and helps them feel confident? These questions don't have simple answers. Like any medium, a combination of factors work together to create an experience. Although our starting point is always scriptwriting, we've identified a number of lessons we learned that go beyond writing and focus on presenting explanations in a manner that befits our audience. The following story highlights our transition from written to video explanations and provides 10 lessons we learned in the process.

Common Craft Gets Started

As mentioned earlier, the first few Common Craft videos were based on blog posts from 2004 that were intended to explain RSS and Wikis to my consulting clients. The blog posts were written explanations, and they were successful at the time. A few people left comments and wrote about them, which was exciting for someone just beginning to blog.

But my articles were not *remarkable* in any way. They may have made a particular idea easier for people to understand, but they were similar to every other text-based communication out there. The medium was effective and showed that I could write a good blog post, but in the end, they were adrift in a sea of millions of articles. As much as I enjoyed creating them, they didn't take on lasting value in my mind.

In 2006, several events occurred that prompted Sachi and I to begin thinking differently about how to share ideas. First, 2006 was the year YouTube rose in popularity—something we watched closely. To us, it represented a transformation that would make big waves in the mainstream audience and we oriented Common Craft around riding that wave.

2006 was also the year we purchased our first video camera and began shooting video in our travels. We would record interesting moments, such as drinking vodka with Russians or getting street food in Shanghai. Then we would edit the footage in the hotel room at night and share it on YouTube. We couldn't believe how cheap and easy it was. Sure, the camera had cost us a few hundred dollars, but video editing software came with our laptop and YouTube was free. Suddenly, we were amateur video producers.

We had fallen in love with video as a medium by the end of 2006; however, we still needed a way to make it a part of Common Craft. This was around the time that we began noticing explanation problems and recognized the great need for someone to explain RSS in a way more people could understand. Soon we remembered those old blog posts, and we began thinking about how they would look in video form.

After a few failed experiments, Sachi hit on the idea of pointing the camera down onto a whiteboard and using hands, markers, and paper cut-outs to tell stories. Within a few weeks we made the first Common Craft video.

At the highest level, we made a conscious choice to use video as the means of making our written explanations interesting and remarkable. We saw an opportunity to transform the written word into a medium that would appeal to our target audience. We learned to present explanations in a new, more effective way.

We also learned a number of lessons from making Common Craft videos along the way, ideas that I hope will help you begin to think about presenting your own explanations. Following is a list of our favorites.

Ten Lessons Learned from Common Craft Explanations

State Your Intentions Early. As I have mentioned, context is an important part of creating an explanation, and perhaps the first chance we have to build context is the title we give our work. As you've likely noticed throughout the book, our video titles are the topic we're explaining, such as "Search Engine Optimization" or "Saving for Retirement," followed by either "Explained by Common Craft" or "in Plain English." This prepares the audience for the presentation and sets expectations. The title becomes a way to show that the video's intention is to accomplish a specific goal.

Solve a Problem. People in any situation—a classroom, business, or a social setting—are anxious about falling behind on information. If you can create an explanation that solves a problem and helps them feel confident about an idea, it will make an impression and create demand for more. We noticed, for example, that social media was plagued with poor explanations, so we oriented our work around solving explanation problems about it.

Keep It Short. People are busy, and their attention spans online—where our videos are most often viewed—are even shorter than normal. This is why we always keep our videos under 4 minutes long, and why they are designed to relate only a handful of ideas. This is one of the constraints that matters most. If a video explanation is too long, the cost to view it becomes too high and people will ignore it. We embrace the fact that we cannot include every detail in such a short time, and instead use the 3 minutes to move someone from disinterest to interest, which can develop into much more.

Reduce Noise. People are surrounded by noise all the time, whether it's that of their coworkers or the visual noise of a complicated software interface. We live with noise so constantly we've gotten used to it. That's why experiences designed to *reduce* noise stand out and attract our attention. We make a concerted effort to reduce visual noise in everything we do. Nothing appears on the whiteboard that isn't there for a purpose. This creates a clean, uncluttered experience for the viewer that feels accessible and simple.

Use Visuals. Many people are visual learners. Although text is the basis of any explanation, the combination of text and visuals can be greater than the sum of the parts. By using visuals effectively (see Chapter 16), explanations can become more remarkable and memorable. They not only create new opportunities to increase understanding by putting two parts of the brain to work at once, but also give your explanation a unique style. Visuals have the potential to captivate the audience in a way that words alone cannot.

Embrace Imperfection. Common Craft videos are inherently imperfect in presentation. They feature hand-drawn characters on hand-cut paper—and we don't always color inside the lines. In contrast to the slick marketing and visual effects that people routinely see, our paper cut-outs feel approachable and disarming—the way a handwritten note seems compared with an e-mail. Within the first few seconds, our videos show that we're more concerned about substance and understanding than polished design and perfection. And that matters.

Slow Down. The first few Common Craft videos were presented with minimal practice, and looking back, it's obvious they were too fast. We performed the voice-overs with sentences that seemed to run together and the visuals moved from scene-to-scene quickly, all of which created a high-intensity experience. Although this made the videos shorter, it prevented some members of our audience from following along and feeling confident. Since that time, we've re-recorded the voice-overs for those early videos. We now approach our current work with an emphasis on a consistent, low intensity pace that appeals to very wide audiences and accounts for a variety of viewers, such as older people and those for whom English is a second language.

Be Timeless. One characteristic of video is that it can portray an event as it happens. Whether it's a sporting event, an interview, or an explanation, video captures and preserves the experience at that point in time. We've learned that this can be a risk as well as an asset because we want our explanations to be valuable today *and* years into the future. If we use an example that changes six months later, the video becomes outdated and less relevant. Some refer to this as *shelf-life*. We've become aware that our explanations can have longer shelf-lives if we focus on big ideas and themes such as blogs or secure passwords rather than specific features, trends, and brands.

Be Accessible. One of the earliest lessons we learned about sharing video was that it presented a challenge to the hearing-impaired. We heard from a number of viewers about the need to reach this population, which is why Common Craft videos are now in a number of formats, including those with captions. In whatever medium you choose, consider the implications for those who might face challenges in experiencing your medium, then try to find a way to make it accessible to them as well.

Have Fun! Gentle humor and informality is one of the true hallmarks of a Common Craft video. Unlike many corporate videos, we make it a priority to not be too stuffy. Often, this means using features such as unexpected visuals, hand gestures, and even sarcasm or facetiousness. For example, in our video "Computer Viruses and Threats" we talk about a type of threat called a *Trojan* and we use the Trojan Horse as an example. At one point in the video, the horse raises his tail and poops a virus. In the often dry world of explanation, this informality helps us be remarkable and hopefully causes people to smile.

Keep these points in mind when thinking about how you'll present explanations. Here they are together:

- State your intentions
- Solve a problem
- Keep it short
- Reduce noise
- Use visuals
- Embrace imperfection
- Slow down
- Be timeless
- Be accessible
- Have fun!

Common Craft's chosen medium is video, and although it works for our audience and goals, it's merely one of *many* types of media that can be used to present explanations in a remarkable way. Because the sheer amount of choices can seem overwhelming, the following chapter will provide you a starting point for evaluating media and using constraints to account for your audience and access to tools.

EXPLANATION AT WORK: KEITH PEARCE AND INTEL, INC.

Keith Pearce has become a star inside Intel for his work in making the complex world of benefits and compensation easier to understand for Intel employees. We've worked with him directly on multiple video projects, and he has become one of our most trusted and respected partners. Our work together with his colleague Michelle James won an IABC Gold Quill Award in 2011. I asked Keith to answer a few questions about his use of explanations inside Intel.

Question: Why do you use explanations in your work? What do they do for you?

I use explanations in two main ways:

1. Making the complex simple.

    Employees at Intel get great benefits, but if you've ever looked at a doctor bill or a health insurance statement, you know that this is not a simple system. How do you help employees understand their complex benefits, not only so that they can really make the best use of them, but also so that they feel great about how their company takes care of them? We use explanations to make the complex simple so that the underlying value becomes more accessible.

    When I was young, we visited Disneyland. It was a memorable trip for me, as it is for most children. But my clearest memory was the visit to the Magic Shop on Main Street. My parents bought me a puzzle box. It was the kind where you have to slide a panel over, then one up, and another one over, and so on, until the box opens. And it only opens if you follow the steps, which are very difficult to intuit. I mean, that's why they call it a puzzle.

    Once, I put money in the box and put it all back together so that the puzzle was re-set. I told my sister that she could have the money in the box if she could open it. Forgoing the discussion about how rotten that was and how I've not changed all that much, the puzzle box can serve as an illustration of making the complex simple.

    My sister couldn't open the box. She tried for a while. Once I called off the bet and explained a bit about how to solve the puzzle, she opened it easily. Fascinatingly, seeing how easy it was to open the box seemed to make her angry. It's like she was saying, "Why did it seem so difficult when it's actually very easy?" For me, it was enjoyable all around.

    Now that I'm an adult, I see so many ideas that are locked up in puzzle boxes of complexity. They appear impenetrable at first. However, with a bit of explanation, the box springs open and the hidden value is suddenly released in a simple form. In this way, learning is the journey to understanding. Explanation leads us on that journey.

Intel employees need explanation—efficient explanation. These are folks who are designing the next generation of technology. And they do it every 18 months, according to Moore's law. That's a fast pace and they generally don't have time away from chip design to learn about health benefits and medical insurance billing on their own. It's not their main gig. It's not how they use their creativity or how they bring their unique gifts to the job. Explanation helps them reap the benefits without sowing from scratch.

2. Innovation and influence.

The other way I use explanation is innovation and influence. In the prior example, I used explanation to build understanding about an existing thing. When innovating, I need to build understanding about ideas or about something that *doesn't yet exist*. I can't get funding for my project unless I can paint a picture of why the idea is good or what value it brings. Explanation puts the paint on the blank canvas.

In my corporate situation, the medium of explanation is PowerPoint. People often rage about PowerPoint, but it's the *use* of PowerPoint that's the issue. In any case, conveying a new idea involves carefully using words, images, patterns, styles, and animations. Two-hundred-seventy-four words crammed onto a single PowerPoint slide is not explanation. It's a misdemeanor (or should be).

Being able to explain, describe, illustrate, and enliven your innovation through clever use of PowerPoint means being able to influence. It's the difference between getting funding or not, between getting executive support or not. Do it poorly and it could mean the difference between the corner office and the corner with a dunce cap. That's not a good look for anyone, frankly.

Question: How do you use explanations? Can you be specific about a couple of use cases?

Intel has a strongly centralized culture and a very well established corporate intranet. We use our corporate portal to share Common Craft videos with our employee population. An employee can be at their desk, connected at a coffee shop, or at home and watch. Short video is an ideal explanation medium for a technology-savvy, busy audience.

We have also used explanatory videos that we developed in group meetings with employees. In one situation, we used a 17-minute video that was broken up into five chapters. After each chapter, we stopped the video and interacted with the audience, taking questions and discussing the information provided. We then started the next chapter, stopped and discussed, and so on. In this way, even more complex information was shared via a longer video but with discussion interspersed to make it easier to assimilate.

(continued)

(*continued*)

Another method for sharing explanations is *waterfalling*. We have an established practice of distributing PowerPoints from a senior leader to his/her staff who, in turn, sends it to their staff, and so on. In this way, explanations encapsulated in PowerPoint are distributed by e-mail. The assumption here is that the explanations in the PowerPoints are, well, self-explanatory. They have to be readable in standalone fashion, sort of like a brochure.

Question: What outcomes do you expect or have you experienced? What have you heard from your audience?

We get very positive reactions about our use of short explanatory videos. People love them. On the other hand, I find that it's rare that someone says, "That's a great PowerPoint slide set," but it does happen. Perhaps the audience knows that almost anyone could have made that PowerPoint but that, for the most part, video is beyond their capability. I find that the art and science involved in making an effective explanation is often completely lost on the audience when it is well done.

The only somewhat negative comment we get about our explanations is that we've "dumbed it down." But, one person's dumbed down is another person's Rubix cube. I accept that our explanations may miss the mark with individuals who already understand the material. In that case, I just assume that the person is not part of our target market. And that's okay. Annoying, but okay.

Although Intel is a very metrics-driven company, we have not as yet attempted to measure in any detailed way the impact of our short videos. We have some ideas for measures and I expect we will get to them eventually. The anecdotal feedback is positive and voluminous, and for me, that's enough for now.

CHAPTER 15

Right Medium for the Message

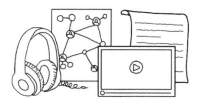

Have you ever wondered about the lack of cooking shows on the radio? They exist, but are few for a very simple reason: this medium is not the best fit for the message. Radio is an auditory medium and cooking is best when it's visual, or even better, live. This mismatch highlights a crucial idea: medium matters.

One of the keys to getting the most out of an explanation is being deliberate about the media in which you choose to present it. It's easy to fall back on sending an e-mail or creating a PowerPoint presentation with bullet points—and who knows, it *might* be effective. But looking at all of our media options allows us to move beyond something that simply works and instead formulate explanations that are remarkable and sharable.

Explanations, by definition, are meant for sharing. In isolation, they wither and die. This chapter is devoted to giving your explanations an opportunity to flourish and potentially, live forever.

A Transformation

As we discussed earlier, explanations often enter the world in the form of text. After planning and packaging ideas, we *write* an explanation to capture the major points. These written explanations are much like a screenplay for a movie or the Common Craft video scripts we've included in previous chapters. The written word is a simple and accessible way for us to explain an idea and communicate it to others. But text is just one of many options for conveying our message to others.

You have multiple options at your disposable for how you can present explanations; so many, in fact, that it can seem daunting. Do you use images, text, audio, or video? Do you put those media into presentation software? An infographic? Webinar? How about recording and sharing it? Can you capture the presentation in a way that makes it useful anytime, anywhere?

These are very important considerations, because—as we addressed at the chapter opening—the medium is likely to help shape the message. The choices we make will influence how the audience will perceive and use our explanation, and even the best-written explanation can fail if we choose poorly.

Before diving in, I think it's important to set the stage because the world of media can be very complex. Media are often combined across platforms and contexts, creating infinite combinations and opportunities. For example, a simple video may include text, visuals, and audio or combinations of each.

As much as I would love to provide a method for matching the perfect media with every situation, it's just not realistic—or possible—to do so. Media decisions aren't and *shouldn't* be prescriptive. Your audience and access to tools are unique to you and the explanation you're crafting. Therefore, the best path forward is to share a range of options and show you how to approach the process in a way that aids your decision-making.

To help us think through these options, let's group them into three big buckets.

1. **Media options**—The various forms of communication
2. **Presentation modes**—The platform that presents the forms
3. **Recording and distribution options**—How we make the resulting explanation sharable

As you can see in the following chart, these three options work together and can be used as a process.

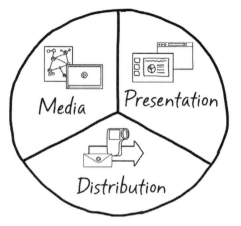

Media Options

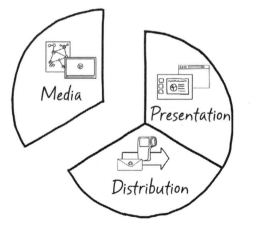

In the following I've provided a succinct look at the popular media that can be useful in presenting explanations, as well as the pros and cons of each. For now, our focus is the form of the communication. What form of media or combination thereof can we use to explain?

Text: The written word; a medium we see in books, newspapers, magazines, e-mails, an so on.

- **Explanation Pros:** Text is often great for exploring a subject with depth and analysis. It is easy and inexpensive to produce and can be very flexible. It works on the Web, on mobile devices and can provide hyperlinks to other resources.
- **Explanation Cons:** Readers often just skim text rather than diving into it, and with today's short attention spans, this can mean that messages don't get through. It's not likely to be considered a *remarkable* form of explanation.

Image/graphic: A visual representation of an idea, concept, person, and so on that is often communicated in the form of a poster or individual graphic.

- **Explanation Pros:** An image or graphic can make complex subjects or data quick to understand and easy to digest. It can also offer the viewer a memorable experience that can be used represent emotion or symbolize an idea. Images and graphics offer a wide variety of options, from infographics about process to scenery that evokes a sentiment. Furthermore, visuals can be uniquely accessible to all languages and reading abilities.
- **Explanation Cons:** Although images and graphics can be hand drawn or produced with software, some complex visuals require graphic design skills and tools. The variety of visual options can feel overwhelming, and they can occasionally create unneeded noise in an explanation. Poorly designed infographics can cause increased confusion.

Audio: A recorded voice or experience that is auditory. An audio recording is what we hear on the radio through podcasts or simply via discussion.

- **Explanation Pros:** Audio is a good storytelling medium and enables the listener to imagine their own versions of what is being spoken. It can be consumed while accomplishing other tasks and excels at relating a person's personality and emotion. When combined with visuals, audio can create a compelling and memorable experience.
- **Explanation Cons:** Audio recordings often require equipment and editing skills to produce, and sound quality is an important factor. Audio is difficult to skim or preview and alone, may not be attractive to the audience. Further, earphones may be required for listening to audio in office situations.

Video: Recorded media including audio, visuals, and movement. We usually see these on TV and in movies theaters and on YouTube.

- **Explanation Pros:** Video is capable of creating a dynamic experience that can engage the viewer for sustained periods. It can capture live-action emotion and body language as well as simple animations and motion graphics. It's very flexible and capable of relating dense or complex information quickly. Video becomes more powerful when combined with an audio experience such as music or voice-overs. Additionally, you can produce it with very simple and accessible tools such as smart phones and presentation software and it is often attractive to the audience.

- ° **Explanation Cons:** Although video can be easily captured, you often need some level of editing software and skills to produce a compelling video product. Voice-overs are an important element in video explanations and can be difficult to perform and edit, and video can be very expensive to produce. Furthermore, high quality video productions can be costly.

Live Demonstration: In-person presentation; what we experience in a classroom lecture or discussion. It involves the use of physical models or some other real-world experience.

- ° **Explanation Pros:** Live demonstration can be an engaging way to present an explanation because it enables discussion and collaboration. The audience is less likely to tune out in this scenario and is better able to understand complex ideas. This form is very flexible, can use all media types, and can be broadcast or recorded. Live demonstration can take advantage of flip-charts and other analog presentation tools.
- ° **Explanation Cons:** Live demonstrations often depend on a presenter who is an excellent communicator. Furthermore, demonstrations are usually limited to the people in attendance and cannot be easily reproduced without video equipment and skills.

From McCombs, 2012.

Presentation Modes

It is likely that your explanation will exist as a combination of the media above. Now that we've covered the basics of each type, it's time to look at our presentation *mode* options. The question now becomes—where will we *put* those media? In what container or platform will the media reside?

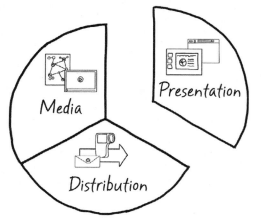

Just like newspaper is a mode for text and images and television is a mode for video and audio, the modes we will consider are suited to some media more than others. Examples include:

Documents: Documents are the primary way businesses communicate information. The most popular are software-based word processing documents and spreadsheets.
- **Explanation Pros:** Documents are a standard and familiar platform for media that most computer users use often. We can use them to communicate explanations in text, data, and images. Furthermore, documents can be easily saved on computers and networks and sent via e-mail and other sharing options.
- **Explanation Cons:** Because documents are such a standard platform, they may not attract attention or interest, and they aren't usually a good fit for multimedia outside of images. Documents, particularly those sent as attachments, are often overused in organizations and may prevent some audience members from engaging.

Presentation/Slideshow: Presentation or slideshow software is used to document and share ideas and concepts in a slide-based format. These are often used for in-person presentations or saved for viewing individually.
- **Explanation Pros:** Presentations are an excellent format for information that is presented linearly, with each slide relating to the next. They are capable of handling multimedia and are a common and familiar platform to most business users. Furthermore, presentation software comes with options for animating visuals and adding voice-overs to create a video experience without the use of cameras or editing software. Presentations can be a great asset in telling stories and creating storyboards. The files can be sent via e-mail and saved to computers and networks.
- **Explanation Cons:** Slideshow presentations have a reputation for being used ineffectively and may turn off some audience members. Presenters often achieve effective presentations by combining good design with their ability to engage an audience. These programs may not work effectively on mobile devices.

Website: Websites offer a very wide variety of options in presenting explanations.
- **Explanation Pros:** Websites are capable of handling almost any media and are the most flexible of the modes listed here. They can offer a worldwide, always-on experience for computers and mobile devices. Websites excel at presenting video and are capable of promoting on-site discussion between viewers. Websites can be easily shared with a URL.
- **Explanation Cons:** Websites require an Internet connection and web browser to work. Although they are flexible, most website experiences require a combination of design and development skills to succeed. Websites can also be expensive and time consuming to produce and manage.

Webinar: Webinars offer the benefits of a face-to-face meeting via the Internet, allowing people in different geographic locations to attend the same meeting. Most webinars are online presentations in which a presenter and meeting attendees use web browsers or software to share a common screen. The audio portion of the meeting is usually provided through calling into a conference phone line.

- **Explanation Pros:** Webinars can be an excellent platform for explanations and are often collaborative; attendees can chat or speak with the presenter and other attendees in real time. Most webinar systems are capable of using multimedia and offer a unique opportunity to see live demonstrations of the websites and software the presenter is using. They are often used in concert with presentation software to conduct training and can be recorded and viewed later.
- **Explanation Cons:** Webinar systems are often expensive and require some training for both presenters and attendees. Webinars are focused on computers and may not work with tablets or other mobile devices. Furthermore, they often require both Internet and phone connections.

Video: Video is both a medium and a presentation mode that combines audio, video, and other media along with movement.

- **Explanation Pros:** Video is a very compelling platform for explanations because it usually combines audio and visual media to create an experience that enhances learning and retention. It is easy to share video on the Web, embed it in presentations, or save it on computers and networks. Videos are also capable of being very attractive and remarkable.
- **Explanation Cons:** Video files are often large and can be difficult to manage, and high-quality video is an expensive option for most. Furthermore, video is difficult to skim and may present accessibility problems for the hearing impaired. It can be challenging to ensure that video will play on all devices and platforms.

Web-Based Presentation Apps: There are a growing number of web-based products and applications that provide alternatives to slide-based presentations tools like PowerPoint. Examples include Prezi and Slide Rocket.

- **Explanation Pros:** These products offer a unique and often remarkable mode for presenting explanations using multimedia and text along with zooming and scrolling capabilities. They can generally be presented via website or in-person. Most products offer a free or trial option and may work well with tablets and other mobile devices.
- **Explanation Cons:** The software can be difficult to learn and in some cases, produce odd side effects like motion sickness when viewed. While free options are available, most require monthly or annual subscriptions for all features. Some applications require an Internet connection.

So far, we've discussed two of the three big considerations: media and mode. This accounts for the variety of media that we can use to display or represent our explanations (media) along with their presentation to the audience (mode). This gives us a solid foundation for thinking about the potential. For example,

- A professor who needs to explain her finding in quantum mechanics may see that a combination of text, images, and live demonstration are the best media options. Furthermore, in presenting she may see that a webinar or slideshow may be good modes.
- A startup founder may envision his explanation in the form of an interactive website that includes text and images that follow the story of a user adopting the product.
- A corporate trainer may wish to share her explanation with customers in real time. Along with her voice, she can use drawings on a flip chart, images and graphics that match her words. A live demonstration or webinar that uses a slideshow may serve as solid modes for this.

The examples are endless. Before getting into how we make these decisions, let's discuss the third consideration: recording and distribution.

Recording and Distribution Options

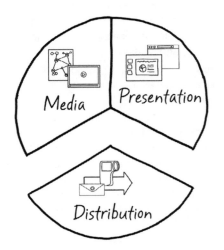

To frame this idea, consider an explanation presented orally in a face-to-face meeting. Once the presentation ends, the explanation disappears, only living on in the attendees' minds. Although this may be great in some situations, it limits the potential of the explanation to reach and impact more people. Thanks to new technologies, we now have better options for capturing or recording explanations that we can then distribute and share, increasing the potential audience and making them more useful and powerful. Recording an explanation gives it the chance to spread and flourish into the future.

The explanation from our previous example could be recorded with a basic video camera on a tripod. This would capture it in a form in which others could share and view it in the future. It's this simple idea that turns a meeting, webinar, slideshow, and so on into a video that can reach many more people.

Another example involves slideshow software such as PowerPoint or Keynote. Although you could record a live presentation with a camera, you could also create the same presentation using the voice-over and animation options that come standard with most presentation software. Again, this approach would create an experience that can be easily captured and spread. As you consider how to present your explanations, don't forget the potential to record it so it can be more widely shared.

Before getting into the short stories that bring these ideas together, let's review.

- **Media options** help us see the options we have in moving from text to other media
- **Presentation mode options** help us see the platforms for sharing our media-rich explanations
- **Recording and distribution options** illustrate the potential to capture an explanation and distribute it to reach a wider audience

It's a lot to absorb and I realize that it may seem overwhelming. However, as you'll see in the following, we have ways to distill all this information and apply it to the realities of our professional lives.

Constraints Come to the Rescue

As constraints have shown us previously, abundance can be paralyzing. Therefore, we need ways to understand the options before us and determine which ones make the most sense for our situation.

Instead of defining the perfect tool for every situation, I think it's more powerful to think at a higher level about the basic options we have and learn to use constraints to help us decide what will work best. Two types of constraints that we'll use are:

Media constraints—These focus on the explainer's access to media.
Audience constraints—These focus on the audience's need and situations.

For a simple and rather extreme case, let's meet Ivan.

Ivan works for a manufacturing company that is making big changes to their line of products. The CEO has asked him to explain the situation to employees. He's spent a few days honing a written explanation and is now trying to determine how to best present it. Before considering all the options on the table, Ivan thinks about two types of constraints:

Media constraints: As a manufacturer, Ivan's company doesn't rely on technology as a communication medium. There is no media department or tool for making videos or audio recordings. There isn't an internal Intranet or the means to produce webinars, and Ivan doesn't have the budget to purchase new tools. These are Ivan's media constraints, and by thinking through them, he can see that he has only a few options.

Audience constraints: More than 80 percent of the company's employees work on the factory floor, speak the same language, and do not use computers regularly at work. All employees work in the same building and often expect to find information from management in their employee mail folders by the break room. Furthermore, the employees work in two shifts and are rarely on site at the same time. These are the audience constraints for Ivan, which help him focus on what is possible for his explanation.

By thinking about these media and audience constraints, Ivan is able to move most of the options off the table and focus on the media that will work for him and his company. Soon Ivan decides that a face-to-face meeting is the best option. In it, he will use presentation software as well as words and images to present his explanation. He'll hold the meeting twice, once for each shift, and provide hard copies of the presentation with notes to each employee.

Although these constraints might initially seem limiting, they actually provide a service to him because he can quickly hone in on the best options by considering the constraints on his audience and media options.

For most readers, this decision likely will be more complex because Internet communication is usually a viable option. Here are a few examples of people who chose to present their explanations by considering media, presentation, and distribution in the context of their personal media and audience constraints.

The Salesperson

Jackie has been selling software for a decade, and now that she's taken another look at the potential of explanation, she's ready to try something new. A few weeks ago she wrote an explanation telling the story of a person using her software. She knows that the explanation works, but she also knows that text isn't the best option.

To start, she considers what likely will make the most sense for her audience—busy executives who move from meeting to meeting and are tired of long, boring presentations. They don't read anything longer than a few sentences; rather, they need a quick and remarkable way to see how her software will change the world.

This tells Jackie that her text explanation probably won't work well, and audio shouldn't be considered. They won't take the time to attend a webinar. But a short video, a graphic, a live demonstration, or an interactive website are all potential options.

Jackie also thinks about the media to which she has access. She can knock out bullet-point PowerPoint presentations all day long, but they may not make an impact. Her company has a media team, but they don't have the bandwidth or tools to make a video. The web team is already behind on their assignments and probably can't build something for her quickly. However, they *do* have graphic designers available.

These constraints bring more focus. Video is out. An interactive website isn't likely. This leaves two options that will fit within the constraints of audience and media:

Live demonstration
Graphic

In the end, Jackie is able to work with a graphic designer to create an infographic that transforms the story in her explanation into a visual that captures the big points in an easy-to-consume and remarkable format. It quickly becomes her go-to resource for grabbing the attention of the busy executives she targets. Now that she has proven it works, she distributes it to her whole team, who make it a part of every pitch.

The Startup Founder

Akira's technology startup company is going to be a big deal someday, but he's currently having a difficult time explaining it to investors and customers. His team has poured everything into development and now he needs a way to get people to care about it. He wrote an explanation that builds context, tells a quick story, and connects his product to ideas his audience already understands to help with this. But he knows his customers don't read much anymore, so he needs a way to make his explanation remarkable.

When he thinks about his audience, he thinks about money. His explanation needs to help him get funding from investors and eventually, revenue from customers. Soon he sees they all have something in common: they are all tech-savvy and spend a lot of time online. They're overwhelmed by all the new ideas and products on the market. They're looking for something remarkable and, above all, easy to understand.

In terms of media, Akira has many options. Although the company is self-funded right now, the team is gadget-oriented, informed about media, and has some very creative members. His media constraints aren't about access so much as effectiveness. Akira knows that investors will expect a slide presentation, and although he plans to create one later, right now he just needs something to get his foot in the door, and that's a tall order. Text, audio, and live demonstrations are all off the table, and a webinar wouldn't make sense. He sees video and graphics as potential media options, along with an interactive website. Akira works with his team to create a strategy for turning his explanation into something that will be useful and remarkable.

A team member has been experimenting with animated video and has the required tools. These videos are all digital—what is known as *motion graphics*. The team decides that Akira could present his written explanation in the form of an animated video. It would be around two minutes long and would combine voice-overs and visuals to tell the story.

After a few weeks the video is complete and looks amazing. Suddenly, it's possible for anyone to see the big idea with a small investment of time. The team then recognizes all kinds of sharing opportunities. They upload it to YouTube, put it on the front page of their website and send links to friends and investors with the promise that it will make their product easier to understand.

Although their video explanation wasn't a viral hit, it did turn people onto their company, and even compelled a few investors to pitch in. That was just the beginning, however. The video became an essential part of every presentation because it was something they could show at the beginning to set the stage. They also used it on the website to invite people to test the product. A call-to-action appeared at the end of the video, inviting viewers to take the next step. Plus, because it was shared on YouTube, anyone could embed it on their website and distribute the message to even more people.

The Trainer

Monica has spent most of her life in front of an audience of learners, first as a teacher and then as a corporate trainer. Now that she's working at a large company, she spends a lot of time on the road training users of her company's product. She's always been a firm believer in the power of *standup training*, in which everyone is in the same room.

Being able to ask questions and share a common view of the product is a huge benefit from her perspective.

Monica was therefore very excited when her manager asked her to lead the training on a new product. She loves the process of instructional design and recently has been working to include explanations as part of her training. But her manager explained that things have changed. Travel expenses are too high and she will not be able to train users face-to-face. Now it's up to her to figure out how to make it work.

It's clear to Monica that the audience has specific needs. They must learn about the new product in a situation similar to a meeting, and they must be able to ask questions and see how Monica uses the product. Her users all work in medium to large companies and always have a computer and Internet connection. Furthermore, they have never had problems making time for training, and most have a good understanding of the big idea behind the product already.

Normally, she wouldn't have to think much about media. Most of her presentations simply display the product on the screen as she steps through the process of using it. But she now has to consider what's workable for this situation. She could e-mail an instruction manual with text and visuals to them, but that wouldn't be remarkable. She needs a medium like a live demonstration—something that happens in *real time*. This will allow her to present her product explanation and have discussions that account for any questions.

It soon becomes clear that a webinar is Monica's best option. She can do almost exactly what she did in-person using the Internet instead. Users would call into a conference line and join an online meeting to see a shared screen. Although this made her a bit anxious at first, she learned to love how effective webinars made her presentations. They reduced her need for travel, thereby allowing her to spend more time with her family.

After using webinar software for a few weeks, Monica noticed a feature she had never used that allowed her to record a webinar. It captured the screen and all the discussion. After trying it, a whole new world opened up. Now she could capture the training sessions and make them available on the company website. This way, anyone who needed a refresher could just watch the recording of their session.

Monica continued to have live meetings, but the ability to capture and distribute them easily meant that she could always point former students to recordings and use her limited time more effectively.

Summary

As you can see from these and other examples, your explanation's success is not based on a single factor. A great written explanation can only go so far. To be truly effective, you'll need to consider how to transform your explanation into forms that fit with your audience and their needs. Thankfully, we have more choices than ever before in how we accomplish this. Although the variety of media at our disposal can seem overwhelming, it's not insurmountable. You can't use a simple formula to find the right combination of media for every situation; however, we can use constraints to help give our explanation a form. By thinking in terms of audience and media constraints, we can narrow the choices to a manageable few that fit our needs.

Next, we'll dive into a chapter that focuses on the use of visuals in our explanations and see how visual thinking can be used to represent ideas and solve problems.

CHAPTER 16

Visuals

In 2004, *Wired* Magazine editor Chris Anderson wrote an article called "The Long Tail," which he adapted into a book with the same title in 2006. From the book description on Amazon.com:

> The Long Tail *is really about the economics of abundance. New efficiencies in distribution, manufacturing, and marketing are essentially resetting the definition of what's commercially viable across the board. If the twentieth century was about hits, the twenty-first will be equally about niches.*
>
> —Chris Anderson, *The Long Tail*

I read both the article and the book when they were published, and they made a big impression on me. More than anything, the idea of the *long tail* gave me a way to think about how the Web is changing marketing and commerce. Once the big idea was clear in my mind, it became a tool that I could use to discuss a company's marketing and distribution strategy. It was a powerful concept that explained one of the Web's biggest impacts on business strategy.

But as you can see from the previous description, words just don't do the idea justice. Let's look at what else has been written about the basic concept of the long tail. The current Wikipedia article begins:

The Long Tail *or* long tail *refers to the statistical property that a larger share of population rests within the tail of a probability distribution than observed under a "normal" or Gaussian distribution. A long tail distortion will arise with the inclusion of some unusually high (or low) values which increase (decrease) the mean, skewing the distribution to the right (or left).*

—Wikipedia, 2012

From Anderson's article:

To get a sense of our true taste, unfiltered by the economics of scarcity, look at Rhapsody, a subscription-based streaming music service (owned by RealNetworks) that currently offers more than 735,000 tracks.

Chart Rhapsody's monthly statistics and you get a "power law" demand curve that looks much like any record store's, with huge appeal for the top tracks, tailing off quickly for less popular ones. But a really interesting thing happens once you dig below the top 40,000 tracks, which is about the amount of the fluid inventory (the albums carried that will eventually be sold) of the average real-world record store. Here, the Walmarts of the world go to zero—either they don't carry any more CDs, or the few potential local takers for such fringy fare never find it or never even enter the store.

The Rhapsody demand, however, keeps going. Not only is every one of Rhapsody's top 100,000 tracks streamed at least once each month, the same is true for its top 200,000, top 300,000, and top 400,000. As fast as Rhapsody adds tracks to its library, those songs find an audience, even if it's just a few people a month, somewhere in the country. This is the Long Tail.

—Chris Anderson, 2004

These descriptions are somewhat helpful and understandable. With no other context, many readers would find the idea interesting and useful. But the *real* power of the long tail is not evident until it becomes visual. Only then does the idea really come alive.

Thankfully, Anderson does provide visual aids in his book and articles, which do a great job of explaining the idea. In the following, I'll walk you through the idea using my own visuals and you'll see how the long tail becomes a simple *visual* tool that captures a way to communicate a powerful and transformational idea.

Let's start with the basic chart, which anyone can quickly draw. It has two axes, with a measure of volume on the vertical axis. This is a measure of information such as sales. The horizontal axis exhibits specific items such as titles or products, with the most popular on the left and least popular on the right. For our example, we'll use sales and products, respectively.

To bring it together, we draw a *power law* or *demand* curve that is steep on the left (the head) and curving down to the right, almost touching the bottom (the tail).

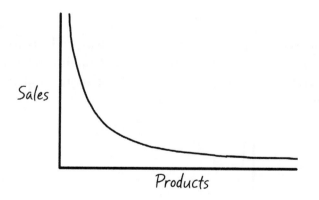

The area under the curve is the visualization of demand. A key point is that the right side of the curve—that is, products with low demand—can be very long. This is the *long tail* of the demand curve.

Products on the left have exponentially more demand than products on the right. For example, in the context of historic record sales, The Beatles and Michael Jackson records are on the left and the long tail of lesser-known bands are on the right.

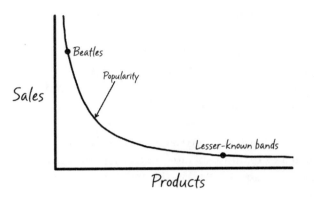

That's it. These three lines give us everything we need to visualize and explain how business has changed since the Internet spawned online retailers with unlimited shelf space.

Let's see how.

Before the Internet, retailers had to choose what products to sell. Visually, this means they had to draw a line on the demand curve and only sell products to the left of that line—those in current demand. They could not afford to offer the products with lesser demand due to shelf space constraints.

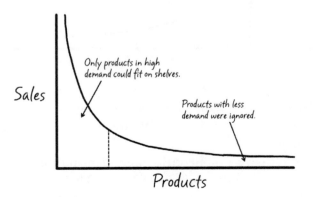

Then the Internet came along and businesses were no longer limited by shelf space, which meant they didn't have to draw a line at all. They could carry products in the long tail—those with very little demand—and offer consumers nearly unlimited choice. Of course, the question then became: will this approach work? Is there enough demand in the long tail to justify carrying so many products?

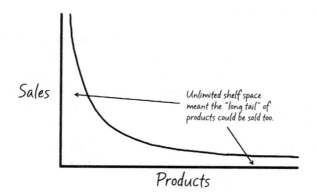

You only need to look at the examples of Amazon.com, iTunes, and Netflix to see the outcome. These retailers have built successful businesses by serving the demand in the long tail.

I use the long tail example here because it's a powerful idea that is difficult to comprehend *without* a visual. As we saw in the beginning of the chapter, words don't always do the trick. Only after we introduce a visual do some ideas easily make sense to the average person. The visual becomes the embodiment of the idea, something memorable and reproducible. And that is the goal of visuals in the context of explanation: they make ideas memorable and reproducible.

Once I read Anderson's article in *Wired*, I could walk into any classroom, spend 10 seconds drawing a simple demand curve, and explain a big way the Web is transforming business. I could plot points on the curve to illustrate case studies and examples. I could use the curve to ask questions and start discussions, and the students would have the same power. They could take the idea and draw it on a notepad at home. They could read the news and visualize how a company's strategy would look on the curve.

Keep the idea of the long tail in the back of your mind as we discuss visuals in this chapter. A simple curve, drawn without artistic expression, is all it takes to give your audience a way to understand and remember an idea that words may not be able to capture.

You Can Use Visuals

People's creative anxieties tend to take over when they begin to consider using visuals in explanations. They automatically say things like, "I can't draw" or "I'm not creative." It's a normal reaction, and it's true that not everyone is an artist. But remember the demand curve and long tail: it comprises three lines—and two of them are straight! Using visuals in explanations is not about art or beauty—it is a utility, a tool for making information clear, just like our explanation scale.

As it turns out, there are simple ways to think about the proper use of visuals in explanations. Like the long tail and explanation scale, they are visual tools that require only the most basic drawing skills. As we'll see in the following, almost any challenge you have can be visualized using one of six basic types of drawings.

Dan Roam's 6 × 6 Rule

Dan Roam is a true luminary in the world of visual thinking, which is probably why his book *Back of the Napkin* is an international bestseller (Dan Roam, 2008). Your first impression may be that visual thinking is about using drawings to represent ideas. Although that's part of it, I'd say that visual thinking—Roam's work in particular—focuses not only on representing ideas but also on solving problems. Drawings are a means to an end in this context. As he says in the book: "Any problem can be made clearer with a picture and any picture can be created using the same set of tools and rules."

According to Roam, you can classify any problem into six *problem clusters:*

- **Who and what** problems—challenges that relate to things, people, and roles
- **How much** problems—challenges that relate to measuring and counting
- **When** problems—challenges that relate to scheduling and timing

- **Where** problems—challenges that relate to direction and how things fit together
- **How** problems—challenges that relate to how things influence one another
- **Why** problems—challenges that relate to seeing the big picture

Much of *Back of the Napkin* is related to solving these problems with pictures, which I've provided here as a starting point for discussing the types of visuals we can use for each situation. My hope is that you'll see the potential to create visuals that help your explanation become more understandable and memorable. Here's a graphic that relates the big ideas:

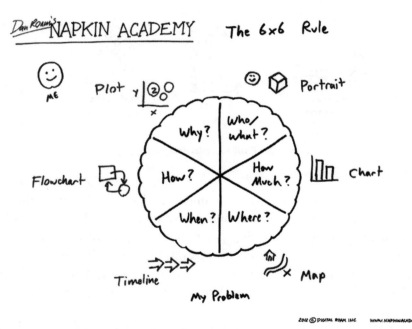

As you can see, the six problem clusters are associated with specific kinds of hand-drawn pictures that best relate that information and solve problems.

Although Roam's book goes into much greater detail, I'll use the example of a startup company that has developed a gadget that helps people track and share their fitness goals. The examples following are meant to help you 1) see the potential of using visuals in your explanations and 2) identify the right kind of visual for any challenge you encounter.

Who *and* What *Problems—Challenges That Relate to Things, People, and Roles*

2012 Dan Roam © Digital Roam, Inc.

A big challenge for the company is to understand their market. Although they have basic data on the target customers and know their general characteristics, they need to define them further. By creating portraits that represent the main user types, they can point out traits and recognizable features using simple drawings. For example, a marathoner could be represented by a stick figure wearing a racing bib, a casual runner could be accompanied by a dog, and the fitness junkie could be shown on treadmill.

These types of representations provide a solid foundation for explanations by making them people- and story-oriented. Each individual uses the product differently and these portraits help highlight that difference in story form.

How Much *Problems—Challenges That Involve Measuring and Counting*

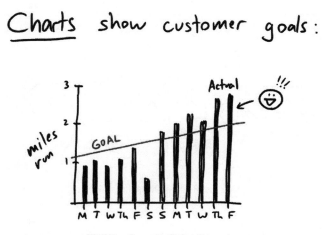

2012 Dan Roam © Digital Roam, Inc.

The company runs on data (pun intended). Their product provides a way for customers to track and share data about their progress toward specific goals, so it's natural for that data to be presented in chart form. Charts are perfect for quantitative data, or data that shows *how much* of something. In the previous image we see customer goals in terms of miles run, which is trending upward and passing the customer's goal in the last week.

Although company leaders recognize the value of charts, they don't always use them when explaining trends and progress toward goals. However, by explaining the company's growth strategy in chart form, everyone can see that the company's financial numbers are a lot like the reports their customers see—they help visually explain why the company is adopting new strategies and goals.

When *Problems—Challenges That Relate to Scheduling and Timing*

2012 Dan Roam © Digital Roam, Inc.

Many people inside the company know that users of the product go through phases of use. They begin by purchasing the product and then progress through a number of steps, each of which has its own characteristics. Although this progression often appears in lists and discussions, people don't often communicate it in visual timeline form.

By creating a timeline of the user's adoption progress, the company can see how the phases fit together and use visuals to explain the characteristics of each phase. For example, phases that last longer take up more of the timeline than shorter ones. In explanation, this allows the audience to see this difference immediately. In the previous example, the team can see that the longest phases are "thinking" and "loving," whereas the phase of trying the product is short. By representing time or duration visually, we have the potential to increase understanding and reduce the words and numbers that can create clutter and cause misunderstanding.

Where *Problems—Challenges That Relate to Direction and How Things Fit Together*

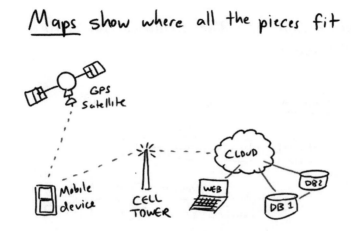

Maps show where all the pieces fit

2012 Dan Roam © Digital Roam, Inc.

This kind of problem may sound like it's related to actual geography, such as how much gas it will take to get from Philadelphia, Pennsylvania, to Chicago, Illinois. Although that can be true, the idea is much broader because it relates to a visual representation of proximity, whether ideas, products, or people. Examples could be Venn diagrams, concept maps, and so on.

For instance, our company could create a map that highlights how the various technologies fit together to make the product work. By mapping out the various tools and hardware, and using visuals to show how they connect and relate to one other, it becomes clear how the system does or does not work. For example, the map illustrated previously shows that the databases connect to the cloud and to each other. A map, compared with text, makes it easier to see and understand how a complex system fits together. It also has the potential to show roadblocks, dead ends, and relationships in a way that brings the big picture to life.

How *Problems—Challenges That Relate to How Things Influence One Another*

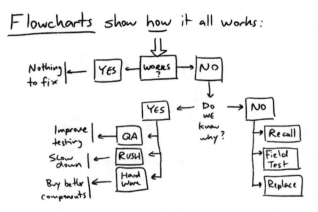

2012 Dan Roam © Digital Roam, Inc.

Like any company, this one is constantly trying to understand and explain why things are the way they are. Let's say we have a bug in the product's software and the cause is unknown. The core question is: how did we get here? Specifically, in this case: how did the software bug that's causing us problems get into the product? The focus of these problems is often cause and effect.

To find the answer, we can start by asking why it happened and representing the answers visually. It could be bad quality assurance (QA) practices, poor programming skills, or rushed timelines. From here, we can zoom in on one cause and dive a little deeper. Why did QA fail? Again, we list reasons. This path of cause and effect helps the company identify how it got to the current situation, and highlights what can be done to fix it.

Why *Problems—Challenges That Relate to Seeing the Big Picture*

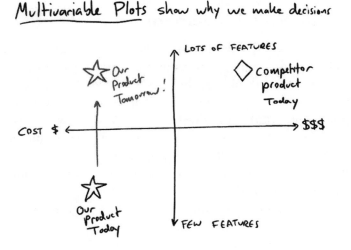

Multivariable Plots show why we make decisions

2012 Dan Roam © Digital Roam, Inc.

Like most, this company is not alone in their industry, and to make smart decisions, they need ways to understand and explain how they compare with competitors. They need to see the big picture across a number of different variables. We can use a multi-variable plot for this—a tool that's both powerful and complicated.

You've likely seen a bubble chart, in which companies are plotted on a diagram with their market share illustrated by the size of their bubble. These drawings are usually based on quantitative data, and are helpful in showing a snapshot of an entire industry or market.

Before heading into an all-hands meeting, the leaders need to explain how the company compares with others in the industry across two important variables. They decide to compare themselves with competitors based on features and cost. Here, the horizontal axis represents a continuum from low to high cost. The vertical axis represents features, again from low to high, which creates four quadrants. The company can then use data to show where they are on the graph compared with competitors. Although they appear in the lower left quadrant (low cost, low feature count), their biggest competitor is in the upper right quadrant (high cost, high features). This creates a big picture view of the industry and allows every employee to see where the company fits.

Common Craft Visual Metaphors

At first blush, Common Craft videos seem to be focused on visual thinking, which I think is a valid point. Visuals are an incredibly important part of the Common Craft experience. We do use visual thinking principles, however, our videos are more focused on the *script* than the visuals, as discussed in Chapter 12. The way we look at it, the visuals support the script, not the other way around. As such, our visuals are often a mix of literal representations (a person sends an e-mail) and more symbolic representations (the Web as an ocean of search results) of ideas from the script. The fact is, every second of a Common Craft video must have a visual and we use a very wide variety of them to create the experience we need.

Below are a few examples of various approaches to using visuals in our video explanations.

Risk

 We wanted our video "Investing Money in Plain English" to illustrate the idea of risk, and we decided to show a choice between two routes to a destination. One route was less risky but took longer. The other was riskier but shorter. This helped us connect investment risk to a real world situation that everyone could understand.

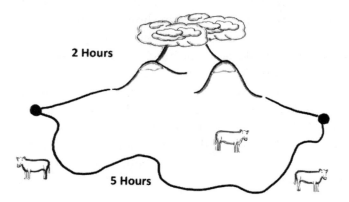

The Smart Grid and Electricity Usage

 The smart grid is a big idea that frames how our electrical grid is evolving to become more efficient and reliable. Whereas the average citizen sees the grid in terms of power lines and electric meters on their homes, much of the grid's functionality remains invisible to us. Our video on the smart grid uses multiple visuals that help us show, as in the example, how the price of electricity changes over the course of a day.

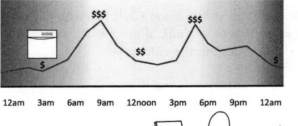

Tweets

 We've made a few videos explaining Twitter, for which we needed a way to symbolize tweets moving around the Web. Because this happens online, we had to find a way to represent a tweet in the real world. We used a simple talk bubble for this. When the bubble appears, a tweet has been posted to Twitter.

My hope is that you'll start to see the problems you face in the context of simple drawings. Think about the kind of problem or challenge that you're explaining when you're working on an explanation. Chances are, you'll be able to represent the problem to others more clearly by considering the options listed previously.

Noise and Simplicity in Visuals

If we zoom in a little and look at Common Craft videos at the image level versus the idea level, it reveals another way to think about visuals. For example, here are a few examples of characters that appear in the videos:

These three figures are no different than any others we use in the video, and they have a pretty obvious feature in common: they don't have faces. We generally do not use facial features, aside from the occasional smile. This is a constraint that guides every figure we draw.

Here's another example. It's the image we use in explanations that involve web browsers:

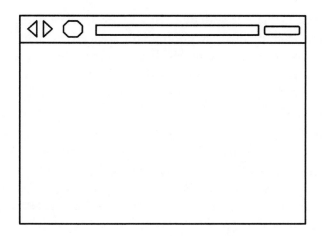

Although it's a very simple version of a web browser, it's enough for people to recognize it immediately. These examples are a part of a strategy focused on achieving simplicity by removing noise. Faces on people, buttons on a web browser—these are noisy in the context of a Common Craft video.

Let me explain.

We may not realize it, but our brains are constantly tuning into other people's emotions and expressions. Whether it's a model's face in a magazine or an old man on a bus, we pay attention, often subconsciously. Part of our brain becomes devoted to processing that information. And it's not just faces; our brain is constantly at work in the background.

Common Craft videos are designed to be a noise-free experience. The figures don't have faces because faces would represent unneeded noise—something for your brain to perceive and understand. By not having faces, we can simply remove that from the equation. But the lack of facial features goes a little deeper.

Long before Common Craft videos, I read an amazing book titled *Understanding Comics* by Scott McCloud. In it, the author makes this point:

> *The ability of cartoons to focus our attention on an idea is, I think, an important part of their special power, both in comics and in drawing generally. Another is the universality of cartoon imagery. The more cartoony a face is, for instance, the more people it could be said to describe.*
>
> —Scott McCloud, *Understanding Comics*, 31.

McCloud's point is that a face drawn with a high level of definition is more likely to look like a specific individual. A photograph is clearly a specific, unique person. But a face drawn in cartoon style removes that specificity. Suddenly, the face could be anyone. By removing features to the point of becoming a smiley face, the specificity goes away completely. A smiley face could be anyone.

McCloud continues:

> *Thus, when you look at a photo or a realistic drawing of a face—you see it as a face of another. But when you enter the world of a cartoon—you see yourself. I believe this is the primary cause of our childhood fascination with cartoons.*
>
> *The cartoon is a vacuum into which identity and awareness are pulled . . . an empty shell that we inhabit which enables us to travel in another realm. We don't just observe the cartoon—we become it!*

And this, of course, is our goal at Common Craft: to have people see *themselves* in the characters we use in the videos. By eliminating faces, we can invite people to do just that.

Screenshots

Many of these ideas are also true for things like websites or software interfaces. We don't use realistic photos or drawings of interfaces because they are so noisy. Here are two examples of interfaces that have appeared in videos:

"Twitter for Business": www.commoncraft.com/video/twitter-business
"Social Networking (Facebook)": www.commoncraft.com/video/social-networking-facebook

Again, these are versions that remove the noise that comes with actual screenshots. By creating our own versions, we can take out elements such as navigation links, advertising, and other features that distract, and instead keep viewers' attention on the ideas that are the focus of the explanation.

When doing so, we ask whether or not the words, faces, buttons, features, or ideas support the big idea or make it more difficult to see. This perspective illustrates what a noisy world we live in. It's so normal to us that the *lack* of noise is what strikes us as strange. Our challenge to you is to be that exception and work to remove noise from your message, giving people a way to experience your ideas without distractions.

Infographics

The thought of visuals is likely to bring to mind a number of ideas for you. I want to be clear that the visuals at the focus of this chapter are a *specific kind* of visual.

In recent years, infographics have become an interesting and often useful way to present information. In most cases, infographics are poster-like visuals that bring information together in a unique and interesting way. Most are quite sophisticated and created by graphic designers or professional data visualizers. Perhaps one of the most famous is by Charles Minard, who used a visual to show Napoleon's disastrous invasion of Russia, 1812–1813.

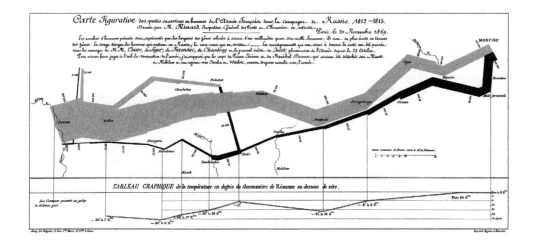

This graphic shows multiple variables at a time:

- **The size of the army**—providing a strong visual representation of human suffering, for example, the sudden decrease of the army's size at the crossing of the Berezina river on the retreat
- **The geographical co-ordinates,** or latitude and longitude, of the army as it moved
- **The direction that the army** was traveling, both in advance and in retreat, showing where units split off and rejoined
- **The location of the army** with respect to certain dates
- **The weather and temperature** along the path of the retreat, in another strong visualisation of events (during the retreat ''one of the worst winters in recent memory set in'') (Corbett, 2012).

I love this visual because the simple use of line width relating to the size of the army is so powerful. However, as amazing as it is, it's not something I recommend trying to replicate for your explanations. If you can, more power to you, but this is a work of genius.

Today's infographics are more likely to be fun and to artistically represent a variety of topics such as fashion trends, technology adoption, and comparisons of data across countries. The following two examples are by a Seattle company called Killer Infographics. The first infographic represents information on the facts and benefits of recycling old cars and the second represents Nikon's history.

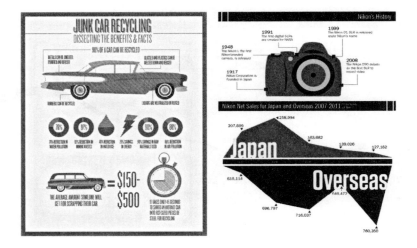

In some ways, they are like one-page explanations. These kinds of explanations can be made in-house with the right design skills. However, it can also be a good investment to hand the idea over to a design company that specializes in data visualization.

Creating Digital Visuals

Most of the ideas in this chapter apply to drawing during a meeting or event, which could involve a whiteboard or legal pad. Although these are valuable and useful, it's sometimes a priority to include your drawings in a PowerPoint presentation, which is digital. I recommend a couple of options for this:

Plug-in Tablet. All Common Craft drawings enter the world in the same way: via a simple tablet that plugs into my computer. I open a drawing program, pick up the pen for the tablet and start drawing. When a drawing is done, I save it as an image (.jpg, .png, or .gif) and then simply insert it into a presentation slide like I would any other image.

Mobile Tablet. Thanks to the growing number of apps on tablets, we're seeing many options for drawing on touchscreen devices such as the iPad. Often, these drawings are done with a stylus that mimics the touch of a finger on the screen. Here again, it's a simple matter of creating a drawing, saving it as an image and inserting it into your presentation.

Scanner. This is how we created images for the first Common Craft videos. Draw an image in pencil on a piece of paper; when finished, use a black marker to make the lines visible. Then, scan the image with a document scanner. This will create a digital version of the image that you can crop and insert into a presentation.

Summary

We're surrounded by visuals every single day, and we take most of them for granted, from watching the stock market to tracking the weather to driving from here to there. It's nearly impossible to imagine a world without visuals. When it comes to explaining our ideas, however, we fall back on what we know and use only the tools we have at our fingertips. Spreadsheets and bullet points are easy to create and have worked in the past. Things have changed, however, and we have greater potential to think about our ideas as visuals that help solve problems and make your explanations remarkable and useful. The key is to get started today. Practice, develop, play. Only by diving in and trying it will you discover the power of visuals in your explanations.

EXPLANATION AT WORK: JULIE SZABO, MARKETING STRATEGY

Julie Szabo is the founder of web marketing agency Capulet Communications. A big part of Szabo's job is helping people understand and feel comfortable with technology, especially social media. As Szabo tells us, ''We've introduced new social web technologies to a lot of companies over the years, mostly marketing VPs and managers who will use social media tools themselves or teach colleagues how to use them. That often includes running training sessions where we need to help participants feel comfortable with new tech and best practices for using them effectively fairly quickly. All this requires a lot of explanation!''

Szabo uses explanations as a way to get people on the same page quickly, which allows her to use her time more effectively. She also sees power in the ability to capture and share explanations with others.

''We often use video explanations in strategy presentations and training sessions to introduce high-level concepts. They set the scene for how and why people use social media. With the basics covered, we can more quickly dive into the weeds.

''We've also produced a number of infographics that express complex data in simple visualizations. We use infographics as compelling visual add-ons to reports or complicated stories that we promote and share with journalists and influencers.''

Szabo echoes the idea that explanations thrive when they are fun and interesting: ''Trainees always enjoy Common Craft explanations, because the videos simultaneously explain and entertain. We work hard to imbue our own explanations with humor and fun. Entertainment is the spoonful of sugar that can make a complex idea palatable.''

''The desired outcome for using infographics is that journalists and influencers share the image and accompanying data with their audiences. Adding infographics to pitches has been a successful tactic for making data more intriguing and sharable.''

CHAPTER 17

Emma and Carlos

When we last checked in with Emma and Carlos in Chapter 13, they were working their way through an explanation problem focused on helping employees at their company learn about a new health care plan. After their last meeting, Carlos had asked Emma for a few days to prepare for their next meeting. Now he's ready.

Once the team filed into the conference room, Carlos started the meeting with a group discussion about movies. He asked the team about their favorites and what they liked about them. After a bit of small talk, he zeroed in on a specific movie two team members loved, *The Shawshank Redemption*. Everyone agreed it was an excellent movie. Carlos used this example to make his first big point.

"Did you know that Stephen King wrote that story as a novella in 1982?" The team looked puzzled and Carlos smiled; he couldn't believe that this example had fallen right into his lap. "Yeah, King wrote it. It was called 'Rita Hayworth and the Shawshank Redemption,' and it was adapted as a movie in 1994" (Wikipedia 2012).

Emma couldn't help saying, "That's great, Carlos, but let's get on with the meeting." He smiled and said, "Oh, this is very pertinent for the meeting today. You see, all of our work on explanation up to this point has been our 'Stephen King phase' of the project. We've created a story in the form of the written word. And like Stephen King's novels, our words have huge potential." He paused and then continued. "But to reach it, we'll need to consider how we can adapt our explanation for other media."

"So does that mean we have to start over?" said one team member.

"No, not at all," explained Carlos. "You see, the movie took Stephen King's story and made it remarkable and memorable by adding visuals and color. It became a new medium that appealed to people in a different way than the written word."

Building to his big point, he said, "That's what we're talking about today. Our explanation is great, but to make it truly remarkable and memorable for our colleagues, we'll need to figure out the best media for our message."

The team loved it. They were going to make their own *The Shawshank Redemption*!

Carlos continued. "In all seriousness, I do want to talk about the choices we have in both old and new media and the ways we can use visuals and capture our explanations in a sharable way.

"Sending our explanation via text in an e-mail may help us reach our goal, but if we're serious about reaching people and being remarkable, we need to think differently.

"First, we need to think about our audience because they will help us narrow down the media that would be useful. For example, if half of our employees didn't use a computer at work, it would inform our choice of the right medium. So, our audience is obviously the company's employees. What can we assume about them?"

As the team spoke, Carlos jotted down the assumptions under the heading "Constraints":

- They all speak English
- They work in multiple U.S. time zones
- Most access computers at work, all with Internet connections and e-mail
- Only half have access to the internal company Intranet
- Most are enrolled in the current company health care plan
- They are very busy
- They don't like adding additional meetings to their schedules
- As a group, they are likely at "F" on the Explanation Scale regarding the new plan

"This is a great start! From looking at this list, I think you can see where we are heading. By understanding our audience, we can start to give the presentation of our explanation a form and shape."

Carlos walked to the whiteboard and said as he drew, "You can think about these assumptions as parts of a container that will hold our explanation. They are constraints that help us define our path. For example, if employees are in different time zones, it matters because a live presentation by the CEO may be hard to pull off."

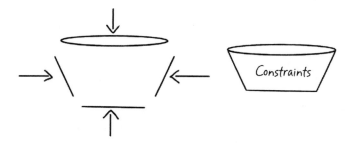

Lightbulbs came on around the room and Carlos smiled. "The more we consider our colleagues' needs and contexts, the more likely we'll be able to present our explanation in a way that appeals to them. So let's figure it out."

The team was now able to agree on a few statements that captured the audience's needs. The members of the audience for our explanation are:

English speaking employees who are likely enrolled in the current health care plan, but lack an understanding of the new plan. These colleagues are very busy and value learning on their own terms. They work in multiple time zones. Most have computer and web access, but limited Intranet access.

The team agreed that these statements were accurate and Carlos drew a simple container on the whiteboard. "We've built a container for presenting our explanation. Now we can think about all our options and see what fits into the container. For example—half of our employees don't have Intranet access. Anything we do must account for that, or it won't fit." The team could see how that made sense.

"Next it's time to brainstorm all the potential ways to present an explanation—and you'll all be a big part of this process," Carlos said as he passed out sticky notes. Over the next hour, the team tried to think of all the media and formats they could use, and grouped related items.

Carlos then went to the whiteboard and said "Let's give these groups names." With a bit of discussion, they created category names like:

- In-person presentations
- Recorded presentations
- Interactive websites
- Webinars
- Videos
- Text
- Audio

After confirming that the list was accurate, Carlos started the next phase: thinking about each medium in terms of the constraints listed previously. Carlos told the team, "We need to whittle this list down to a few options that make sense and fit in our container. And keep in mind that we can use more than one at a time."

"Let's start with audio—does anyone think we should explain the new plan with a podcast or recorded audio?" Heads shook, and with a quick mark that option was off the table.

"What about with text?"

Emma shook her head. "Been there, done that." The team agreed that it's difficult to get busy people to read anything, and when they do, they skim. But one team member pointed out that they shouldn't discount text because some people prefer it over anything else.

"Interactive website?" The team thought about the audience and realized this wouldn't work because half the employees don't have access to the company Intranet. That one was out, too.

"In-person presentations?" The team could imagine these being effective; but they all understood the feeling of dread that arises in most people when they hear about HR presentations. The right presentation could work, but getting people to *show up* was the real issue. Also, because employees worked in different time zones, holding one big meeting would be difficult.

A handful of compelling options were left and Carlos wrote them clearly on the board:

- Recorded presentations
- Webinars
- Videos

All three of these fit with audience needs and could be used to present the explanation. Because they had the text version of the script finished as well, they know they could always make that available.

After a break, Carlos was ready to move on to the next big phase. Now that the team had identified a few options, it was time to think about the overall experience. What would the employee see or experience? How long would it take to view?

Carlos invited the team members to put themselves in an average employee's shoes. "Imagine you're busy with your work but also curious about the new health care plan. What would help you feel informed and confident? How would you *want* to learn? What would be remarkable?"

The team members jumped right in with the first big point. "It would have to be short—less than 5 minutes to learn the basics."

"Good point," said Carlos as he scribbled on the board. "What else?"

"It would need to be on my time. I don't want to have to schedule it," said another team member.

"Awesome—anything else? How would it look? How would you like to see the information?"

"Oh, no bullet points and tiny words on a slide." The whole team laughed; they knew this format all too well.

"Oh, and don't try to say it *all*. Just help me see the big picture." Carlos nodded as he wrote this last idea on the board.

The vision was starting to come together and Carlos summed it up. "So, what if we were able to take our written explanation and present it to employees in such a way that it's 3 minutes long, is focused on the big ideas, is always available, and is presented without bullet points and tiny font—would that work for you?"

Most of the team was enthusiastic and ready to get started, but there were a couple of dissenters, including Emma and the health care plan expert, who voiced their concerns.

"The way you describe it sounds great, and I think you could be onto something. But are we really going to go through all of this for something that's 3 minutes long and only relates a few big points?"

Carlos saw this protest as an opportunity to circle back to the core idea of explanation. "That's true, and I agree that we *could* go deeper; but I also want you to keep in mind that a prerequisite for learning the new plan's details is people's ability to understand and see the *big picture first*. If we can make people care about it in 3 minutes, they'll be motivated to learn more. That's our goal here—making people care."

Carlos then referred back to the written script and encouraged the team to read through it.

"If you look at the explanation in this form, you can see that it works as-is; however, we've already discussed why we're not using it in this form. Like a book that becomes a movie, we'll need to adapt these ideas into a form that will work for our medium."

"Before going further, I want to talk about something I think will help our process. Someone made a point earlier about bullet points, which is something we should keep in mind. I'm proposing that we try to use visuals that work with the words, creating a different kind of experience—something more effective and remarkable."

Of course, some team members couldn't help jumping in and saying, "I think it's a great idea, but who here is an artist or designer? I can't draw."

Again, Carlos was prepared and took a few minutes to give the team a quick tour of visual thinking and how very simple drawings such as the following could be used to present information and solve problems. Before he was finished, people were already thinking about how charts, maps, and timelines could be used to talk about the new plan. They were on their way.

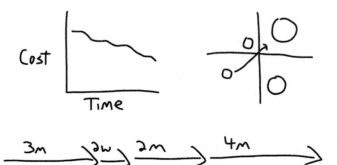

As the team adjourned for the day, a couple of members volunteered to start working on a prototype for their explanation. With Carlos's help, they created images for the story's main characters and the big ideas of the new plan. In looking at the available tools, they experimented with PowerPoint and learned how to animate images and time the visuals to appear as the words were spoken. They also learned how to record a voice-over in PowerPoint that plays along with each slide.

In the end, they were able to use the tools they already had in their office to create a 3-minute PowerPoint presentation that worked much like a video. Once the presentation began, a voice-over guided the viewer through the explanation, with visuals appearing and slides advancing automatically. The first version was a little rough, but it was enough to share with the team.

As a test, Carlos decided to send the explanation to the team just as employees would receive it—in e-mail with an attachment. He even wrote the e-mail message in a style he thought would appeal to employees:

Subject: New Health Care Plan—Explained in three Minutes
Team members,

As you've likely heard, the company is changing health plans soon. To help explain the plans quickly, see the attached presentation, which plays like a video and is only three minutes long. It will help you understand the basics and what the new plan may mean for you and your family. Don't have time now? Save it to your computer and watch it when you have a chance.

If you'd like to read the same information, the transcript of the explanation is below.

Within minutes, he started to get replies from team members. "Fabulous!" "Remarkable!" "It works!"

Carlos was ecstatic. It was only a test run, but it was clear the team was onto something. He reviewed his colleagues' constraints and could see that it fit with their needs. It was short, could be viewed at any time, focused on big ideas, and didn't depend on the company's Intranet. Plus, it used visuals and a format that few had seen before, which made it even more remarkable.

After a few more weeks of experimenting, the team was ready. Their visuals and voice-overs were cleaner and more understandable than ever. At the end of the presentation they included a call-to-action to e-mail their HR contact to get started with the new plan.

Emma was there with Carlos, gritting her teeth before clicking send. She needed this to work to show results to the CEO, who wanted at least 50 percent of employees to sign up for the plan.

With a click, it was sent and they both exhaled. Emma smiled and gave Carlos a fist bump.

"Well, it's up to the employees now. Let's hope this works." She said. Carlos was confident it would.

Epilogue

The new health plan explanation was a resounding success. Although it took a team process to create the explanation, Emma exceeded the CEO's goal of 50 percent of employees registering for the health care plan in six months. Even more importantly, however, she, Carlos and the team were able to introduce the entire company to a new way of thinking about communication. Before then, it had never occurred to their colleagues to focus on explanation problems, much less figure out how to solve them. Now that almost everyone in the company had seen their explanation, they could hardly keep up with requests for more explanations. Suddenly, everyone wanted to create one for their project or product, and Carlos saw a new opportunity: maybe he could be the Chief *Explanation* Officer.

For that, he knew he'd need a *really* good explanation.

CHAPTER 18

Explanation Culture and Your Life as an Explainer

Throughout this book, we've worked to define explanation and put it into practice. We've learned about the curse of knowledge and discovered how context, stories, connections, and descriptions are all tools we can use to make ideas easier to understand. These are not just tactics; they're a way of approaching information and communication. Hopefully, you now have confidence in your ability to explain an idea.

You have the potential to become known as an explainer—someone who has built up their explanation skills and is ready to use them to solve problems. In some ways, this means building a type of *brand* within your organization, team, or even family—a specific brand of communication that focuses on making ideas easier to understand. My hope is that every organization will see the potential to take a step back and consider the role of explanation in how the organization communicates. For that to happen, however, people like you need to push the envelope and make explanation a priority. To see how to do this, consider the following story.

Meet Naima, an executive assistant to the CEO at her company. Naima recently learned about the art of explanation and feels confident that she can make a difference in how her company communicates.

Being a member of the executive suite has given her access to a wide range of projects and ideas working their way through the company and has made her quite adept at identifying explanation problems. Because she's naturally soft-spoken, she's not one to make big proclamations in meetings and therefore hasn't been very effective in helping others see the problems she does. Although she'll often suggest a new way to frame an idea, she's careful not to push too hard. It's a source of anxiety for her because she knows she can make a difference.

Naima and her CEO were having an informal conversation when he mentioned that one of their newest products wasn't being adopted as quickly as he hoped. In a supportive but confident tone, she said this could be because it needs a better explanation. He smiled and agreed without giving it much thought. After a short lull in the conversation, she decided to go for it. She took a deep breath and dove in.

"Explanation isn't just a word; it's a way of approaching how we communicate ideas products and services that makes them easier to understand." The CEO was visibly interested. He had never thought about explanation as a skill, much less as a way to solve problems.

"What do you mean, Naima? Are you saying there is a skill set for explanation— like a specific way to do it well?"

Excited, she replied, "Yes! It's possible to take a bunch of information and package it into an explanation. I've been reading a lot about it." Naima could hardly believe it was working.

The CEO thought for a second and said "I want to know more—set up some time next week for us to dive into this idea one-on-one." It was really happening— she was going to help the CEO see the potential of explanation. Hands still shaking, she made the appointment and started planning.

Naima was excited when the day for the meeting came, but she also knew she had to walk the talk. Her goal was to explain explanation and she did just that. She introduced the curse of knowledge and discussed how to define explanation and why giving a good explanation is so difficult. She made statements that they could agree were accurate and framed the macro view of the world. She built context and made sure that he saw the forest before the trees. She told a story of how explanation solved a problem for someone like him. She used the whiteboard to introduce him to the explanation scale and plotted the company's customers on it.

By the time Naima was done, the CEO was blown away. He sat back in his chair and said, "Naima, how long have you known about this? Why didn't you tell me sooner?" She could only shrug her shoulders. He continued, "This needs to be part of how we do business. I think it could help internal teams, salespeople, and the content on our website. Do me a favor and set up a meeting with the Chief Marketing Officer and present exactly what you did today, OK?"

"Of course," she replied. She was on her way.

A few weeks later, Naima had met with all the executives and a number of department heads and given them all the same explanation of explanation, and most saw the opportunity. Naima's colleagues were beginning to see her as a subject matter expert—someone who held the key to turning data, facts, and information into explanations. As her confidence grew, so did the idea of explanation within the company. What was once a simple word became a way of thinking about communication—a fundamentally new approach.

Naima recently attended a meeting with executives and saw it all come together. After a review of a product's disappointing performance data, the executives discussed explanation as a way turn the product around. In a statement that Naima will never forget, the CMO said "This product clearly had an explanation problem. People aren't adopting it because we're not explaining it well; don't you agree, Naima?"

She smiled and nodded. It was clear that explanation had become a kind of brand within the company. It was considered a business practice and the lessons

(continued)

(*continued*)

about it were well known, but the real power came from the fact that it represented a new and better way to communicate; a way that had the potential to touch every person and idea. Her next goal was to show that the company could explain their way to a competitive advantage.

This example shows not only how Naima successfully presented an explanation, but also presented an idea that represented something new and different, something that demanded attention and cut through the noise. She made the idea of explanation remarkable and made others feel that they could be remarkable as well.

Your Life as An Explainer

If nothing else, my sincere hope is that this book helps you think about explanation as a powerful—and often forgotten—form of communication. Simply thinking about explanation can help you become a better explainer and introduce others to the idea that explanation is a skill that they can both learn and improve.

I want to live in a world with better explanations and to get there, I need your help. As the world grows more complex, the demand for explanations will increase, creating incredible opportunities for people who make explanation a priority. The more people who focus on explanation, the more we can show what a powerful force it is, and how it can help solve real problems.

I want professionals of all types to understand the form and function of explanation so they can not only use it, but demand it. I want a product manager in a company to stand up in her meeting and say, "This needs an explanation." I want a high school teacher to take the facts from a textbook and package them with the intention of creating an explanation for his class. I want *you* to be that person—an explanation specialist.

Explanation isn't just a way to approach communicating an idea, however. It's also a strategy for your career. To see what I mean, I'd like to introduce you to Neil deGrasse Tyson, PhD, the director of New York City's Hayden Planetarium. You might have seen Dr. Tyson's television appearances on *The Daily Show with Jon Stewart* or *Real Time with Bill Maher*. As well as being incredibly smart, his charisma and personality translate well to television.

I bring up Dr. Tyson because he is an amazing explainer, although he may not call himself that by name. A reason he is invited to be a guest on these shows is because he is able to take the complexities of the universe and explain them in a way that invites people to care. Dr. Tyson is so passionate about his work that his explanations are overflowing with excitement and emotion. He sincerely cares about physics, and he makes his ideas infectious by explaining his work in simple terms. He has the combination of very deep knowledge and the ability to account for the curse of knowledge, making his explanations useful and appropriate for almost any audience.

But I want to talk about Dr. Tyson in the context of his profession—a physicist. We all depend on scientists like him for helping us understand the world around us. Like any professional, he cares about his field and wants to see it grow. He wants to see projects funded and young people pursuing a career in physics. He wants to see his profession be successful and productive.

Of course, he's in a unique position to help this cause. By becoming a media figure, he's able to promote the power and spirit of his profession to a mainstream audience. It's not just *that* he makes appearances, however; it's *how* he does it. I see Dr. Tyson as an ambassador for his profession, one whose explanations invite people to care. By turning the invisible world of physics into ideas that inspire, he's able to help accomplish a goal for everyone in his field: to invite new people to be involved, whether that's through funding, research, or simply attention. By explaining his profession, he is able to provide a service to it. And that's my challenge to you.

Every profession, every job title, every role needs at least a few Neil deGrasse Tysons—and I don't mean someone to appear on television and make Uranus jokes with Jon Stewart. I'm talking about making people care about what you do by explaining it better. I'm talking about the potential for you to be an ambassador for your job or profession—someone who can use communication skills to invite people to take an interest in your job and see it from a new perspective.

Although this goal may not increase funding for your profession or impact the number of young people pursuing it, it could have wonderful local results. I previously mentioned explaining my way to the creation of a new job title at my company, and this is just one example. Consider ways you can put this book to work in making your work more visible and interesting, whether it's among colleagues, your family, or your friends.

The next time someone asks you about what you do, see it as an opportunity to explain your job, project, or product from a new perspective. They may ask, "What do you do?"; instead, answer the question, "Why should I care about what you do?" By thinking about your own life and work in terms of explanation, you can start to develop and evolve stories and connections that are more powerful than any answers you've given before.

You don't have to wait around for the perfect explanation problem—your first explicit explanation may be right in front of you. If you seize the opportunity, you may find that it takes on a life of its own. Imagine being interviewed for a promotion or new job and being able to explain your experience in a completely unexpected and impactful way. Imagine being able to teach your peers a better way to explain their projects. Imagine your parents not only understanding what you do and why it matters, but explaining it accurately to their friends. These are not trivial uses of explanation.

More than anything, I hope that I've helped explanation become a new, more useful concept in your mind, because that's the big idea. Once explanation becomes a part of your communication toolbox, you'll start to see all the ways you can use it. I've provided a number of ideas and methods to approaching explanation; however, none of them matters more than the simple realization that explanation represents an amazing opportunity to make your ideas more understandable. If you choose to pursue it, it could change your life for the better.

ACKNOWLEDGMENTS

First and foremost, I want to acknowledge my wife Sachi for her role in this book and, indeed, in everything I do. She operates behind the scenes by choice and although my name is on the cover, this book was a collaboration that could not have happened without her.

We also want to thank our friends and families for always being supportive and interested in our work. They are usually the first to see our videos and play a huge role in improving them. Jay Fienberg and Anastasia Fuller of Juxtaprose built our book website and are a constant source of advice and encouragement.

Of course, Common Craft members and our past clients have motivated us to always learn and to keep pursuing the idea that better explanations are useful and possible. This book would not have been possible without them.

Over the course of writing this book, I contacted a number of authors and experts in the communication world. They each graciously helped me prepare for the process of writing and often provided gems of insight that helped me see new potential. They include Monique Trottier, Dave Gray, Noah Iliinski, Julie Szabo, Darren Barefoot, Patrick O'Keefe, Ian Devier, Sunni Brown, Jay Rosen, Tania Lombrozo, Austin Kleon, Dan Roam, Nancy Duarte, Scott Berkun, and Jessica Hagy.

Many thanks also go to our editors at John Wiley & Sons, including Lauren Murphy, who originally contacted me about this book two years before it was published.

LINKS TO COMMON CRAFT VIDEOS

Throughout this book there are multiple references to Common Craft videos. These videos can be viewed for free on the Common Craft website using the links below.

Author Note

QR Codes Explained by Common Craft
www.commoncraft.com/video/qr-codes

Chapter 2

Plagiarism Explained by Common Craft
www.commoncraft.com/video/plagiarism
Twitter in Plain English
www.commoncraft.com/video/twitter

Chapter 4

Dropbox Video and 25 Million Views
www.commoncraft.com/dropbox-video-and-25-million-views

Chapter 6

Stock Markets in Plain English
    www.commoncraft.com/video/stock-markets
Google Docs in Plain English
    www.commoncraft.com/google-docs-plain-english

Chapter 7

Wikis in Plain English
    www.commoncraft.com/video/wikis

Chapter 8

Augmented Reality Explained by Common Craft
    www.commoncraft.com/video/augmented-reality
Podcasting in Plain English
    www.commoncraft.com/video/podcasting

Chapter 9

Web Browsers Explained by Common Craft
    www.commoncraft.com/video/web-browsers

Chapter 12

Social Media in Plain English
    www.commoncraft.com/video/social-media
BitTorrent Explained by Common Craft
    www.commoncraft.com/video/bittorrent

Chapter 14

RSS in Plain English
www.commoncraft.com/video/rss
Computer Viruses and Threats Explained by Common Craft
www.commoncraft.com/video/computer-viruses-and-threats

Chapter 16

Investing Money in Plain English
www.commoncraft.com/video/investing-money
Twitter in Plain English
www.commoncraft.com/video/twitter
The Smart Grid Explained by Common Craft
www.commoncraft.com/video/smart-grid
Twitter for Business Explained by Common Craft
www.commoncraft.com/video/twitter-business
Social Networking (Facebook) Explained by Common Craft
www.commoncraft.com/video/social-networking-facebook

ABOUT THE AUTHOR

Lee LeFever is the founder and chief explainer of Common Craft, LLC, a company known around the world for making ideas easier to understand via video explanations. The company's videos have been viewed more than 50 million times online, and Lee has worked with companies such as LEGO, Intel, Ford Motors, Microsoft, and Google to explain their products. He lives with his wife and business partner Sachi in Seattle, Washington, where he is often seen with a bouncy, wet dog named Bosco. Follow Lee on Twitter (and other online services) @leelefever and @commoncraft.

Photo credit: Rasmus Rasmussen

BIBLIOGRAPHY

Anderson, Chris. 2004. "The Long Tail." *Wired Magazine.* Issue 12.10 www.wired.com/wired/archive/12.10/tail.html?pg=2&topic=tail&topic_set=. Accessed December 15, 2004.

Anderson, Chris. 2006. *The Long Tail: Why the Future of Business is Selling Less of More.* New York: Hyperion Books.

BrainyQuote. 2012. "Albert Einstein's Quotes." www.brainyquote.com/quotes/quotes/a/alberteins383803.html. Accessed May 17, 2012.

Chi, M.T.H., M. Bassok, M. Lewis, P. Reimann, and R. Glaser. 1989. "Self-Explanations: How Students Study and Use Examples in Learning to Solve Problems." *Cognitive Science* 13: 145–182.

Chi, M.T.H., N. de Leeuw M.H. Chiu, and C. LaVancher. 1994. "Eliciting Self-Explanations Improves Understanding." *Cognitive Science* 18: 439–477.

Corbett, John. 2012. "Charles Joseph Minard: Mapping Napoleon's March, 1861." www.csiss.org/classics/content/58. Center for Spacially Integrated Social Science. Accessed April 28, 2012.

Duarte, Nancy. 2010. *Resonate: Present Visual Stories that Transform Audiences.* Hoboken, NJ: John Wiley & Sons.

Hays, Mathew. October 23–29, 2003. "A Space Odyssey." *Montreal Mirror* 19, no. 19. www.montrealmirror.com/ARCHIVES/2003/102303/film1.html. Accessed June 15, 2012.

Heath, Chip, and Dan Heath. December 2006. "The Curse of Knowledge." *Harvard Business Review.* http://hbr.org/2006/12/the-curse-of-knowledge/ar/1. Accessed June 15, 2012.

Heath, Chip, and Dan Heath. 2007. *Made to Stick: Why Some Ideas Survive and Others Die.* New York: Random House.

Hooper, S. 1992. "Effects of Peer Interaction during Computer-Based Mathematics Instruction." *Journal of Educational Research* 85: 180–189.

Gaffney, Elizabeth, and Benjamin Ryder Howe. 2012. "David McCullough, The Art of Biography No. 2." *The Paris Review.* www.theparisreview.org/interviews/894/the-art-of-biography-no-2-david-mccullough. Accessed May 17, 2012.

Iyengar, Sheena S., and Mark R. Lepper. 2000. "When Choice is Demotivating: Can One Desire too Much of a Good Thing?" *Journal of Personality and Social Psychology* 79, no. 6, 995–1006.

Kean, Sam. 2010. *The Disappearing Spoon: And Other True Tales of Madness, Love, and the History of the World from the Periodic Table of the Elements.* New York: Little, Brown and Company.

Lehrer, Jonah. November 13, 2011. "Need to Create? Get a Constraint." Frontal Cortex [Blog], *Wired.* www.wired.com/wiredscience/2011/11/need-to-create-get-a-constraint. Accessed June 15, 2012.

Lombrozo, Tania. 2012. "Explanation and Abductive Inference." In *Oxford Handbook of Thinking and Reasoning,* edited by K.J. Holyoak and R.G. Morrison. Oxford, UK: Oxford University Press.

McCloud, Scott. 1994. *Understanding Comics: The Invisible Art.* New York: HarperCollins.

McCombs, Regina. 2012. Ideas Adapted from Work via Faculty for Multimedia and Mobile at the Poynter Institute. St. Petersburg, Florida.

McKee, Robert. 1997. *Story.* New York: HarperCollins.

Merriam-Webster. "Explanation." [Definition].

Pearce, Keith. May 31, 2012. Interview.

Roam, Dan. April 20, 2012. Interview.

Roam, Dan. 2008. *Back of the Napkin.* New York: Penguin Group.

Roscoe, R. D., and M.T.H. Chi. 2008. "Tutor Learning: The Role of Explaining and Responding to Questions." *Instructional Science* 36, no. 4, 321–350.

Rosen, Jay. 2008. "National Explainer: A Job for Journalists on the Demand Side of News." *PressThink.* http://archive.pressthink.org/2008/08/13/national_explain.html. Last updated July 17, 2008. Accessed August 8, 2008.

Ross, J., and J.B. Cousins. 1995. "Giving and Receiving Explanations in Cooperative Learning Groups." Alberta Journal of Educational Research 41: 104–122.

Schwartz, Barry. 2003. *Paradox of Choice: Why More Is Less.* New York: Ecco Press.

Szabo, Julie. May 2, 2012. Interview.

This American Life. 2008. "The Giant Pool of Money." www.thisamericanlife.org/radio-archives/episode/355/the-giant-pool-of-money. Accessed May 17, 2012.

Tompkins, Al. 2011. *Aim for the Heart: Write, Shoot, Report, and Produce for TV and Multimedia.* 2nd ed. Washington, D.C.: CQ Press.

Wikipedia. 2012. "Alien." http://en.wikipedia.org/wiki/Alien. Accessed June 15, 2012.

Wikipedia. 2012. "Blog." http://en.wikipedia.org/wiki/Blog. Accessed April 28, 2012.

Wikipedia. 2012. "Explanation." http://en.wikipedia.org/wiki/Explanation. Accessed April 28, 2012.

Wikipedia. 2012. "Long Tail." http://en.wikipedia.org/wiki/Long_Tail. Accessed April 28, 2012.

Wikipedia. 2012. "Rita Hayworth and Shawshank Redemption." http://en.wikipedia.org/wiki/Rita_Hayworth_and_Shawshank_Redemption. Accessed April 28, 2012.

INDEX

Abstract ideas reformatted, 80
Accessibility, 153
Accuracy vs. understanding, 105, 110
Act, 9
Act and art, 11–12
Adoption problem, 38
Agassiz, Louis, 12
Agreement, 49, 127
Agreement and context
   connection, 129
   description, 130
   problem/pain and vision of solution, 129
   realization of solution, 130
   story, 129–130
   story beginning, 129
   vision of future, 129
Alien (movie), 84, 92
Analogy vs. metaphors, 89
Anderson, Chris, 173, 175, 177
Animated video, 169
Animation options, 165
Assumptions, 39, 40, 105, 110
Assumptions, failure from, 24–26
Audience constraints, 166
Audience needs, 48
Audio, 160
Augmented reality, 90–91

Back of the Napkin (Roam), 78, 178–179
Basic language, 105, 110
Big ideas, 122, 132, 142–143, 152–153
Big picture, 58
"BitTorrent by Common Craft," 129
Blank stares, 23
Blog, 67–68
Blumberg, Alex, 13
Brainstorming process, 118
Brand of communication, 203
Browsers, 96–97
Building context, 60
Bullet points, 193. *See also* PowerPoint

Capulet Communications, 194
Caring, 19
Category names, 198
Cause and effect path, 184
Charts, 200
"Chemistry Way, Way Below Zero" (Kean),
   80
Choices, 114
Common Craft
   explanations, 194
   stories, 71–73
   "Twitter in Plain English," 17
Common Craft Style, 21

Common Craft videos, 45, 74, 85, 121, 128
  getting started, 149–151
  lessons learned, 151–156
  noise-free experiences, 189
  storyline, 63
Common Craft visual metaphors,
        186–188
  risk, 186
  smart grid and electricity usage, 187
  tweets, 187–188
Communication brand, 203
Communication culture, 26
Communication forms, 8–9
Communication strategy, 36
Communication toolbox, 208
Comparisons, unflattering, 87
Computer technology, 85
"Computer Viruses and Threats," 153
Concept maps, 183
Conclusion, 49
Confidence
  all about, 24
  building, 40, 55, 92, 95
  explanation(s)affects on, 32
  loss of, 53
  from reminding, 139–140
Connections
  about, 83–84
  analogy, 89–90
  building vs. establishing, 87–89
  Common Craft videos, 90–91
  connecting ideas, 88–89
  establishing new ideas, 88
  on explanation scale, 92
  to ideas, 84
  old vs. new, 84–89
  use of, 49
  summary, 92

Constraints
  about, 113–115
  audience and media, 166, 171
  benefits of, 113
  Common Craft and, 115–117
  example of, 196–198
  and explanations, 117–119
  importance of, 116
  medium as, 165–171, 198
  to process, 115
  summary, 119
Context
  about, 51–53
  beginners then experts, 57–61
  building, 61, 140
  connections, 128
  descriptions, 128
  in explanation, 61–63
  explanation scale, 65–66
  forest then trees, 53–56
  foundation built on, 52
  function of, 49
  Google Docs, 63–65
  as kingdom, 52
  and pain, 63
  presentation without, 55
  problem/pain and vision of solution,
        127
  solving problems of, 56–61
  story, 127–128
  summary, 66
Cost
  of building context, 60
  of connection, 88, 92
  of education and explanation(s), 13–14
  of negative impression, 59
  of poorly explained ideas, 34–35
  of presentation, 58–59

of understanding, 13, 139–140
of video length, 151
Craik, Kenneth James Williams, 20
Cultural adaptation, 79
Culture, 78
Curse of knowledge, 25, 27, 32, 38, 39, 46, 103, 104, 134, 135, 137, 203, 205

The Daily Show with Jon Stewart, 206
Data visualization, 193
Davidson, Adam, 13
Decision making process, 115
Declarative statements, 61–62
Definition, 8
Demand curve, 174–175
Descriptions
    about, 93–95
    explanation scale, 99
    explanation vs. recipe, 97–99
    function of, 8
    how vs. why fuunction, 49
    web browsers, 95–97
    summary, 99–101
Design company, 193
Details, 105
Details and exceptions, 110
Direct approach with no context, 30–32
The Disappearing Spoon: And Other True Tales of Madness, Love, and the History of the World from the Periodic Table of Elements, 80
Documents, 162
Drawings
    simple, 200
    six types of, 178
Dropbox, 41–42
Duarte, Nancy, 118
Dumbing down, 47
Duration, 117

Early adopters, 36, 38
Einstein, Alfred, 27
Elaboration, 8
E-mail
    as analogy, 89
    coordination with, 73
    explaining, 85
    problems with, 64–65, 86
Empathy and explanation, 10
Explanation problems, 34, 37, 132, 134–135
Explanation scale, 135
    descriptions, 99
    how questions, 56
    how-why curve, 94
    introduction to, 36–40
    for packaging ideas, 45
    why questions, 56
Explanation strategy start, 145
Explanation(s)
    affects on confidence, 32
    as art of showing why, 16
    bringing together, 131–145
    connection making, 83
    and constraints, 117–119
    cost of education and, 13–14
    definition, 9–10
    described, 7–22
    describing facts, 133
    from different perspectives, 93
    and empathy, 10
    end of, 128
    vs. facts, 30
    failure of, 23–32
    generating vs. receiving, 22
    highlighting vs., 89
    and learning, 21–22
    make people care, 16–22

Explanation(s) (*continued*)
    preparing and writing. *see* Preparing and writing
    vs. recipe, 97–99
    on right side, 136
    secret to crafting, 130
    as a skill, 4–5
    stories used in, 74–75
    as toolbox, 208
    as way to package ideas, 14–16

Facts, 11
Facts vs. explanation(s), 30
Fact-telling vs. storytelling, 68–69, 70, 143–144
Factual statements, 133
Failure
    from assumptions, 24–26
    of explanation(s), 23–32
    root causes of, 23–24
    of understanding, 26–27
Ferdowski, Arash, 41
Figures of speech, 90
Filtering process, 118
Forest then trees, 205
Forests vs. trees, 55
Format, 115, 117
Fun, 153

Geek perspective, 104
Geeks, 103
Glass, Ira, 13
Google Docs, 84, 86
Gopnik, Alison, 21
Groupon, 84, 86
Guidelines vs. rules, 117

Harvard Business Review, 25
Heads-up display, 91
Hearing impaired, 153

Heath, Chip, 25
Heath, Dan, 25
Heider, Fritz, 20
Highlighting vs. explanation, 89
Houston, Drew, 41
How, 94
    focus on, 94
    vs. why, 99
How much problems, 178, 181
How problems, 179, 184
How questions on explanation scale, 56
How-why curve explanation scale, 94
Human wrapper, 74
Humor, 153

Idea volume, 117
Ideabuilding, 92
Ideas, 115
    already understood, 105
    connections to, 84
Identifying explanation problems, 34–42
Illustration, 9
Image animation, 201
Image/graphics, 160
Imagine How Creativity Works (Lehrer),
    116
Imperfection, 152
Infographics, 160, 168, 191–193
Informality, 153
Ingredients, 98
Innovation and influence, 155
Instruction, 8
Intel, Inc., 154
Intentions stating early, 151
"Investing Money in Plain English,"
    186
iPad, 193
IT bubble, 105

James, Michelle, 154
Jargon, 26–27, 47, 135
"Jaws in Space," 84, 92
The Journal of Personality (Margue), 116

Kean, Sam, 80
Keynote, 165
Killer Infographics, 192
King, Stephen, 195–196

Language, 107, 115, 117
Learning to run, 3–5
LeFever, Sachi, 11, 33, 34, 71, 80, 150
Lehrer, Jonah, 116
Lessons learned
    accessibility, 153
    fun, 153
    imperfection, 152
    noise reduction, 151–152
    solve a problem, 151
    speed, 152
    state intentions early, 151
    timelessness, 152–153
    video length, 151
    visuals usage, 151–152
Live demonstration, 161, 170
Location, 117
Lombrozo, Tania, 19–20
Long tail, 174, 175
The Long Tail (Anderson), 173

Made to Stick (Heath and Heath), 25
Mapping, 183
Maps, 200
Margue, Janina, 116
McCloud, Scott, 189–190
McCoullogh, David M., 12
McKee, Robert, 126

Meaning, 69
Means of production, 11
Media constraints, 166
Media options, 165
Medium
    about, 157
    as constraint, 198
    constraints, 165–171
    importance of, 157
    options, 159–161
    presentation modes, 161–164
    recording and distribution options, 164–165
    transformation, 158–159
    summary, 171
Memorization, 53
Metaphors vs. analogy, 89
Minard, Charles, 191
Mobile tablet, 193
Moore's law, 155
Motion graphics, 169
Movies, 83
Multiple variables graphic, 192
Multi-variable plots, 185
"Murdering your darlings," 118
Music, 115
"Need to Create? Get a Constraint" (Lehrer), 116

Netflix, 84
New concepts, 87
Ni, Albert, 41
Noise reduction, 151–152

O'Bannon, Dan, 84
Organizing process, 118

Packaging, 48
Packaging ideas, 45–49
    about, 45–46

Packaging ideas, *(continued)*
  elements of, 48–49
  outside the bubble, 46–48
Paradox of Choice (Schwartz), 114
Pearce, Keith, 154
People
  as explanation, 70
  and ideas, 51
Personification, 74, 75, 80
Perspective, 12
  broadest possible, 105, 110
Plagiarism, 14–16
Planning explanation(s), 33–37
Planning process, 33
Plug-in tablet, 193
Podcasting, 86
Power law demand curve, 174
PowerPoint, 163, 165, 168, 201
Preparing and writing
  about, 121–122
  big ideas, 123
  Common Craft writing process, 122
  real thing, 128–130
  research and discovery, 123–125
  script writing, 125–128
Presentation, 148
  mode options, 165
  modes, 161–164
  options, 198
  without context, 55
Presentation/slideshow, 162
Prezi (app), 163
Principles vs. rules, 94, 126
Probability distribution, 174
Problem clumps, 178
Problem solving, 151
Process, 9
Process explanation, 78

Product bubble, 47
Project duration, 115

QR codes, 95
Quality assurance (QA), 184

Real time demonstration, 170
Reasons, 16
Recording and distribution options, 164–165
Recording webinars, 170
Report, 9
Representations, 180
Research and discovery, 122
Resonate (Duarte), 118
Rhapsody, 174
Rita Hayward and the Shawshank Redemption (King),
    195–196
Roam, Dan, 78, 178–179
Roam's 6 × 6 rule, 178
Rosen, Jay, 13–14, 19
Rules
  vs. guidelines, 117
  vs. principles, 94, 126

Scanner, 193
Schwartz, Barry, 114
Scott, Sidney, 84
Screenshots, 190–191
Script, 121
  elements of basic, 126–127
  and story telling, 74
Script writing, 122
  about, 125–127
  agreement, 127
  call to action, 128
  context, 127–128
  realization, 128
  story, 127–128

Scudder, Samuel, 12
Self-explanation effect, 22
Shawshank Redemption (movie), 195–196
Shelf-life, 152
Shusett, Ron, 84
Simplification, 100, 103–111, 154
6 × 6 rule, 178–186
Slide Rocket (app), 163
Slideshow, 164
Slideshow software, 165
Smart appearance, 28–30
Smiley faces, 190
Social media, 124
"Social Networking and Facebook," 190
Social networking website, 77
Social Psychology (Margue), 116
Solutions, 40
Speed, 152
Spielberg, Stephen, 84
Spreadsheets, 193
Standup training, 169
Stepping stones to learning, 139–140, 142
Stone, Biz, 17
Stories, 49, 143
    about, 67–68
    basic format, 75–77
    basic format of basic, 75–77
    character introduction, 127–128
    Common Craft and, 71–73
    effects of, 77
    in explanation, 74–75
    explanation scale, 81
    limits of, 77–79
    personification, 73–74, 79–80
    storytellers, 69–71
    summary, 81
Story (McKee), 126
Storyboard phase, 122

Storytelling
    vs. fact telling, 68–69, 70, 143–144
    methods of, 67–68
    romanticized versions of, 69
    and script, 74
    time limits, 78
Substance, 69
Szabo, Julia, 194

Technical accuracy vs. understanding, 88
Term familiarity, 53
The Terminator, 90
Text, 160
The Giant Pool of Money, 13–14
This American Life (Glass), 13
Time constraints, 199–200
Time limitations
    in storytelling, 78
    of storytelling, 79
Timelessness, 152–153
Timelines, 117, 182, 200
Tompkins, Al, 69, 70
Transformation
    distribution options, 157
    media options, 157
    medium, 158–159
    presentation modes, 157
Trees vs. forests, 52
Twitter, 17, 18, 187
"Twitter for Business," 123, 190
"Twitter in Plain English," 17, 18
Tyson, Neil deGrasse, 206–207

Understanding
    vs. accuracy, 105, 110
    vs. technical accuracy, 88
Understanding Comics (McCloud),
        189–190

Understanding failure, 26–27
Understanding scale, 37

Venn diagrams, 183
Vernacular, 46
Video from written form
  about, 195
  category names, 198
  constraints, 196–198
  presentation options, 198
  Shawshank Redemption example, 195–196
Videos, 62–63, 160–161, 163, 165. *See also*
      Common Craft videos
  duration, 115
  explanation, 41
  length, 151
  metrics of, 156
  projects, 63
Virtualization, 103, 104–105
  guidance, 110
  type of, 108
Visual learners, 152
Visual metaphors, 186–188
Visual thinking, 200
Visuals
  6 × 6 rule, 178–186
  about, 173–178
  and color, 196
  Common Craft visual metaphors, 186–188
  creating digital, 193
  ease of use, 178
  infographics, 191–193
  noise and simplicity in, 188–191
  screenshots, 190–191
  special kind of, 191
  summary, 193–194
Visuals usage, 151–152
Voice-overs, 161, 201

Waterfalling, 156
Weaver, Sigourney, 84
Web browser use, 98
Web browsers, 95–97, 188–189
Web-based presentation apps, 163
Webinars, 163, 164, 170
Websites, 162
We-can-all-agree-statements, 140
What if statements, 127
"When Choice is Demotivating" (Schwartz), 114
When problems, 178
Where problems, 179, 182, 183–184
Who and what problems, 178, 180
Why and how division, 137, 138
Why does this make sense focus, 140, 141
Why problems, 179, 185–186
Why questions, 16, 134
  establishment of, 63
  on explanation scale, 56
Why to how, 126
Why vs. how, 78, 98–99
Wiki in Plain English, 71
Wikipedia, 9, 71
Wikis, 71
Wired (magazine), 116, 177
Word count limits, 125
Written word, 121

YouTube, 150

Become an Explanation Rockstar!

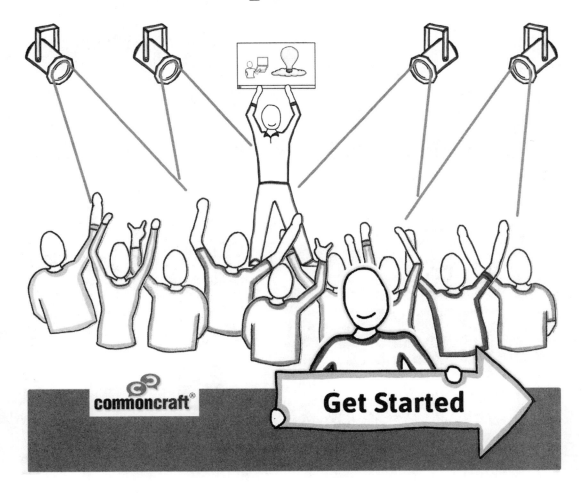

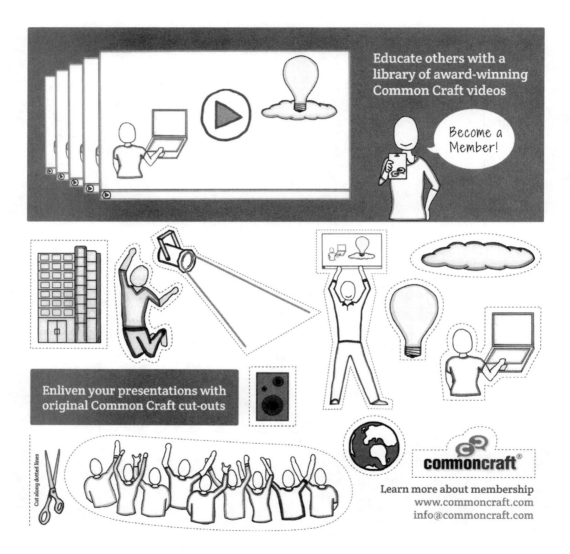